Digital Brand

eCommerce Playbook for Distributors

How Distributors Can Win Online against the National Competitors and Amazon

Justin King

Sarah Falcon, Jason Hein, Ashley Lillis, Kristen Lohman

ISBN 978-0-692-17434-0

To my wife, Beth: thanks for supporting me every step of the way. And also to my four daughters and future entrepreneurs: Sarah, Lauryn, Lainey, and Audrey. You are digital athletes even at your young ages.

To my entire team at B2X Partners: you are B2B eCommerce rock stars, and I couldn't have done this without you.

Contents

FOREWORD

We are living through a period of fundamental transformation in the B2B space. Nearly all selling channels have been digitally-disrupted. B2B buyers can and do defect with one click. And price and inventory information are in the free and clear for anyone to see.

Like their B2C brethren before them, B2B companies are reacting to the seismic shifts by transitioning from single channel and offline-only companies to multi-touchpoint, omnichannel companies. And as with their B2C predecessors, B2B companies are reinventing their value propositions, services, and go-to-market strategies.

But having covered B2B eCommerce for 6 years at Forrester before starting my own B2B strategy firm and co-founding B2B Next (the leading B2B eCommerce event in the world), I can tell you that today's distributors in particular are struggling with the current landscape. Many are challenged like never before to compete against a surging Amazon. Most face ever-rising customer expectations and unpredictable customer loyalties. And a growing number of distributors are engaged in hand-to-hand combat to avoid a spiraling race to bottom on pricing.

Tomorrow's successful distributors must be today's serious players in the digital space. For distributors that are just getting started with eCommerce, it's all about having the right vision and roadmap. For B2B distributors with more mature digital footprints, the game is all about tuning the strategies and tactics.

Justin King and his team at B2X Partners have created a compelling and systematic framework for any distributor looking to compete in eCommerce. It's a straightforward, action-focused approach that addresses the complexities and opportunities available in the B2B digital space. Digital newcomers as well as professionals will walk away with an understanding of how they can transform their businesses into world-class digital enterprises.

I'm excited for this book to debut.   It's a serious piece of methodological scholarship and includes powerful lessons learned and hard-earned best practices. I recommend it for B2B distributors, digital professionals, and eCommerce practitioners of all stripes.

Andy Hoar

INTRODUCTION

It all started with the statement "I don't know what I don't know." The CEO of an industrial distributor said this to me a few years ago after a keynote address I gave to an association. He continued, "Listen, Justin—I believe what you're saying. To survive, we must embrace digital and eCommerce in our business. However, we just don't know where to start, what to do when, what technology to select, whom to hire, and how to manage this new channel." This was the first of many times I would hear the phrase "I don't know what I don't know." That simple phrase started a quest to build a system to help distributors (and, more importantly, their owners) through their digital transformations.

I've seen businesses at all stages of digital development—from green-screen order entry to sophisticated, highly customized eCommerce websites. What connects each business is a core challenge: customers are expecting more and more online, and organizations need a system in place to help meet that challenge. After working with over fifty distributors of all sizes, we developed a system called the **X eCommerce System,** or **XES** for short. Since launch, this system has transformed how distributors understand and implement their digital business.

At B2X Partners, we talk about your digital experience in a simple term: the Digital Branch™. Like your brick-and-mortar branches, your Digital Branch requires planning, resources, technology, and products. Unlike your physical branches, your Digital Branch can be a scalable growth engine to your business. Your Digital Branch opens opportunities for optimization, analysis, and marketing that can be fast, responsive, and constantly forward-moving. Beyond that, opening and driving your Digital Branch is critical for your business to stay relevant and competitive.

But launching a successful Digital Branch isn't easy. Here are just a few examples of how we've seen businesses struggle:

- A distributor decides to implement eCommerce. The head of IT leads the project to build the website. The website is highly customized to its customers' pricing and catalogs but is very hard to use. Adoption is low. Leadership concludes, "Maybe eCommerce works in other industries, but in ours, customers aren't interested in buying online."

- To invest more into its digital business, a distribution company hires a VP with a background in business-to-consumer (B2C) eCommerce. While initially enthusiastic, the new VP is quickly overwhelmed by the amount of new information needed to understand the company's customers, services, and products. The VP answers leadership questions with jargon and evasion—and it takes eighteen months for the company to remove the individual. The company has lost eighteen months of developing its Digital Branch.

- A distributor launches its first eCommerce website – marketing the site to customers and promoting the launch with offers, swag, and events. Six months after the launch, management learns that their lead salespeople are telling customers: "Sure, you can use our website to research, but just place orders with me—I can get you the best price." eCommerce sales remain low.

- The head of marketing of a distribution company selects a software platform for the eCommerce site. The platform vendor sold the software on its functionality, user-friendliness, and modern bells and whistles. The platform never successfully integrates with the distributor's enterprise resource planning (ERP) systems. The website project stalls after two years and over $500,000 in costs.

- An eCommerce website launches. Everyone is thrilled with how the website functions and the fact that it is mobile friendly. However, after the effort of launch, no team is put in place to manage the site, so website content and product listings quickly become out of date.

From the outside, seeing these problems—and maybe even identifying solutions—is easy. Any big digital undertaking will encounter stumbling blocks along the way, and we can't promise that this book will prevent every misstep. But with a clear system in place, you can understand the mechanics of your Digital Branch business—quickly identify issues, challenges, and opportunities— so that you can avoid some of the mistakes we've seen before.

The **X eCommerce System** is about shining a light on your business, best practices, and opportunities so that you have the power to make fast, clear, and forward-thinking decisions to drive your Digital Branch. In describing this system, we break out the seven components critical to a successful Digital Branch. While it's not easy, it is doable. More importantly, it is necessary in order to stay relevant and competitive in a world that is becoming more and more digital.

CHAPTER 1

X eCommerce System (XES)
Get a Grasp on Your Digital Business

Built upon our years of creating profitable, B2B eCommerce businesses, the **X eCommerce System** is a seven-component approach to building a successful Digital Branch. The XES includes the information and resources you need to drive your eCommerce business—from strategic plan, to your website technology, product data, design, and analysis—all centered around providing a customer-centric Digital Branch. By customer-centric we mean orienting your Digital Branch **and your business** around making your customers' work life better.

Each component isn't a silo—it's part of a collaborative effort to provide exceptional customer experience. Harald Fanderl, a partner with McKinsey & Company, describes this approach well:

> *Customers are relatively simple, right? ... What creates the complexity is the company. Through the years, for many reasons, sometimes a new IT system, sometimes regulation, some legal requirements, and so on, add complexities little by little. Because companies do not focus that much on...customer journeys, you end up with an extremely cumbersome experience for customers, which is actually not optimized for the customer, but optimized for the company. What we are advocating now is this shift in perspective, so that the customer becomes the center of attention again.*
>
> **—Harald Fanderl**[1]

In short, Fanderl's message is this: your business needs to be in the business of providing an exceptional customer experience. It's not touchy-feely; it's good business. This is an area where every business can learn from Amazon's mission "to be Earth's most customer-centric company."[2]

As you go through the **X eCommerce System**, don't base your next steps on what your business can do. Rather, focus on being intensely curious about what your customers actually want. For every component, we recommend asking yourself this question: **"How can I build this to make my customers' job faster and easier?"**

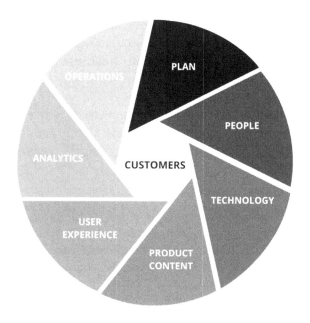

Is B2B Different from B2C?

- ✓ **Favorite Question #1:** Isn't eCommerce just eCommerce no matter the industry?
- ✓ **Favorite Question #2:** Why can't I just get a Shopify shopping cart?

These are great questions that we'll need to answer before we do anything else.

We can learn a lot from B2C. Honestly, the internet is full of information from B2C, and how it can be applied to B2B. The phrase typically used is the "consumerization of B2B." Consumerization of B2B essentially involves your buyers bringing expectations to how your site should work based on their at-home shopping experiences. That conditioning creates expectations that you need to meet in the online customer experience.

However, as you know, your customers' expectations of your eCommerce business are likely different. Unlike their Amazon paper towel purchases, they need detailed product information, their contract pricing, and the branch availability. While they want to be able to search and quickly find their most relevant products, they don't (necessarily) need to see "what's hot now."

The Buyer versus the Shopper

The single, biggest difference between B2B and B2C revolves around this statement:

> *B2B customers and buyers come to your website because they have to. It is their job.*
>
> **—Justin King**

It's a job they do every day, nine to five. In his book *How to Win at the Sport of Business*, Mark Cuban writes that in the workplace more than anywhere else, people look for the path of least resistance. That means your site needs to be about making your customers' job easier. We are all lazy in some aspects of our job. We all have tasks we hate doing but have to because we are paid to do them. How can you website make those jobs a little bit smoother, faster, easier?

If their job is easier on your site versus your competitor's, they will come back. When they come back, they will spend more.

Four Core Challenges for B2B (versus B2C)

Distributor eCommerce is a complex business. You have complex products, complex technologies, and complex customers. B2B is different from B2C. Here are a few of the core challenges:

- **Technological complexities:** An eCommerce platform needs to plug into complex existing systems: the ERP, contracts and pricing, taxes, punchout, product content, workflows, etc.

- **Resourcing:** Finding the right people is difficult. While eCommerce is a hot industry and a lot of talent is out there, those people are often working for cool brands or agencies. It's hard for distributors that may be located outside bigger cities and in industries that aren't as "hot" to find great talent. Also, the products sold in B2B are often not "sexy" to those outside the industry. Worse, outsiders may not even understand what these products are or what they do.

- **Culture shift:** Digital is a big change in the way B2B does business. For organizations that are entrenched or resistant to change, building a Digital Branch represents a change in the demands on leadership and the entire team. Focusing on customer experience will require an integrated effort throughout the organization.

- **Purchasing process:** Procurement in B2B is usually very different than in B2C. B2B buying typically involves multiple people, different departments, and complex approval workflows—meaning additional transparency about buying decisions is more important. In B2C, only your roommate knows what you buy; in B2B, your boss might have to approve each order.

In short, B2B is drastically different from B2C, and taking the complexities and challenges inherent in B2B and trying to fit them into an eCommerce solution built for retail is *really hard to do*. That is why we created the **X eCommerce System**.

How Is Your Digital Branch Performing?

Before we get started, we want to make sure we're on the same page. Do you know how your Digital Branch is performing? To help you assess this, we've created twenty questions that will help define your overall performance.

Rate on a scale of 1-5 (1 is absolutely not, 5 is absolutely yes).

		3	4	5

1. We have a clear plan for our digital experience.

2. We have buy-in throughout the organization for a DigitalBranch.

3. We have a budget to drive the DigitalBranch.

4. We know the people we need to drive the online business.

5. We have the people in place to drive the online business.

6. We have the right technology in place to drive our online business.

7. We know the technology we need.

8. We are currently tracking data analytics.

9. We are using data to drive business decisions throughout the organization.

10. We have sufficient product content on our website.

11. Our product content is optimized for our customers.

12. We can provide a single, consistent price to customers.

13. We have a plan in place to provide a single, consistent price to customers.

14. We have customer service in place for eCommerce.

15. We have a marketing program to drive eCommerce.

16. We understand how to run our Digital Branch as a separate Profit and Loss Statement (P&L).

17. Our organization is set up to support inventory and fulfillment for eCommerce.

18. Being a customer-centric business is a core value.

19. We implement tools, services, products, and content based on a customer experience perspective.

20. We understand what our customers need from an online experience.

Add each number. If your score is:

This system was created for you

35-49% You're normal and not alone; this system will help you rise above

50-64% You are above average and you understand

65-79% You are well above average

80-100% This is your goal

A Start-Up within Your Business

If, like many distributors, eCommerce is a younger division in a larger, older organization, it can be hard to understand how your Digital Branch is performing as a business channel. If that's a challenge in your company, think about treating your Digital Branch as a start-up within your organization—with its own mandate, its own team, and its own Profit and Loss Statement (P&L). This puts the ownership of the Digital Branch into the hands of the operators—where revenue can be separately tracked, and spending is tied directly to the eCommerce business. There are a few innovative businesses that have taken this approach:

- Gamut.com was started as an online-only business launched by Grainger. With a proprietary information system, the site built a robust catalog of product data and focused on elevating products and product sales over branding. Since its launch in 2017, Grainger's overall revenue from online sales continues to increase, and functionality and user experience features from Gamut.com are adopted on Grainger's own eCommerce site, Grainger.com.

- Supplyhouse.com is an online-only distributor of plumbing, heating, and HVAC. Launched under the current name in 2014, the site innovates in customer experience and eCommerce growth. Their digital focus allows them to develop content, marketing, and delivery services focused on driving online sales.

- TruPar.com is an online-only parts business started as an independent project of TruPar America. A bootstrapped start-up, the site features nearly eight million SKUs online and is focused on developing automated solutions to serve its over forty-five thousand B2B online customers.

Seven Components of the X eCommerce System

As you know, eCommerce is not "set it and forget it" – it's a complex system of technology and people that work together to grow your Digital Branch. The **X eCommerce System** was created to break this down into clear, actionable components that apply to every stage of your business's maturity.

Its purpose is to give you a clear understanding of how to leverage every component—whether you're starting at day one or are ten years into the business. We look at seven components of a successful Digital Branch, each centered around your current and target customers: plan, people, technology, user experience, analytics, product content, and operations. In the following chapters, we'll delve into each component.

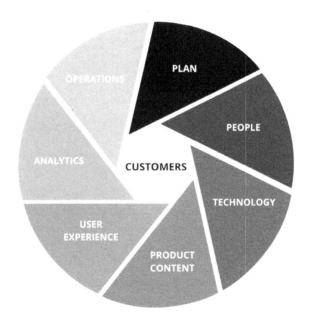

CHAPTER 2

Customers

At the Center of the System

Jan Moore, an entrepreneur, says, "Nothing happens until someone sells something. And nothing is sold until you have a customer to sell it to."[3] Without customers, there is no business. Therefore, we start the XES at the center: the *customers*.

One of the favorite questions we hear is "Why are our customers spending their money with us rather than with our competitors?" This question signals that the distributors have started thinking about their customers behavior (rather than their business needs). Amazon, with its goal to be the most customer-centric business, has this question deep at its core. In order to answer this question, we must understand what motivates the customer. To appreciate the power of the XES, we must understand more about why and how customers buy what you sell.

First, we must understand why people buy.

In the 1950s, William Schutz created a theory of human behavior known as FIRO (Fundamental Interpersonal Relations Orientation).[4] According to this theory, there are three main interpersonal needs that people seek: affection, control, and inclusion. Edgar Papke says it this way: "Customers want: attention, competency, and caring."[5] When customers' needs are met, they feel good. When they are not met, customers get frustrated and angry.

In the B2B world, customers are trying to complete their job. They want reliability and quality (competency), they want to feel like they are important (attention), and they want to be treated well (caring).

Each customer will likely prefer one out of the three. Your company will also meet one of these needs more than the others. In his book *True Alignment*, Edgar Papke says, "Often, we define customer experience without fully understanding it, which is why companies become misaligned with their customers' expectations. Companies must explore the full scope of that experience to understand how to deliver to it."[6]

Do you understand your customers' general preference? Is your company aligned to that preference? Most B2B customers prefer either competency or attention. At B2X Partners, we reach out to distributors' customers and ask: "Why do you buy from Distributor ABC?" In more than three thousand surveys and interviews, we've seen a gap between what the company sees as its strengths and what the customers perceive and value.

Using a word cloud, these are the phrases we hear from distributors themselves when asked, "Why do your customers buy from your company?":

When we ask customers, "Why do you buy from this company?" they respond:

Your task: Understand your customers' needs. Align your business and your Digital Branch with those needs.

CHAPTER 3

Plan

What To Do Today, What To Do Tomorrow

We have seen more eCommerce projects than we'd like to admit start with the technology rather than a plan. A good salesman, an impatient CIO, or an impulsive founder finds a software platform and thinks: "We need to go online and buy this, and that will get it done." While we are sympathetic to those impulses, your approach to a Digital Branch has to begin differently: it must start with a strategic plan.

If you aim at nothing, you will hit it every time.

—Zig Ziglar

If any of the following situations describes you and your business, it's time to get proactive and develop and implement a plan for your Digital Branch.

Top Ten Reasons Why You Need a Digital Branch Plan

1. You feel like you're spinning your wheels and are directionless.
2. Your customers are buying online, and existing or start-up competitors are enjoying that business.
3. Your website lacks a powerful online value proposition/identity.
4. You approach eCommerce as simply a "technology thing."
5. Your business isn't integrated; your digital platform operates in a silo.
6. You feel like you're spending real money but not gaining an advantage.
7. Your digital support team doesn't have enough people/budget.
8. You can't answer the question "What's next?"
9. You're continually playing defense—being reactive rather than proactive.
10. You're rationalizing success.

The Heart of the Matter

At its very core, your Digital Branch is a way of differentiating your business from your competitors and providing customers with a reliable and user-friendly way of buying from you. Your plan identifies how to achieve that—and how to make your Digital Branch better, more profitable, and more customer serving.

This is critical in today's increasingly digital age, as confirmed by the following well-known marketing mogul and entrepreneur:

> *Make your product easier to buy than your competition, or*
> *you will find your customers buying from them, not you.*
>
> **—Mark Cuban**[7]

So, how do you accomplish this? Here are a couple of basic questions to consider when approaching and developing your online presence:

- **What is a Digital Branch strategic plan?** A Digital Branch strategic plan is a written document that includes
    - a clear vision,
    - objectives for your Digital Branch, and
    - metrics to define when objectives are achieved.
- **Where are you today?** Begin with a current-state **analysis** to identify strengths, weaknesses, and capabilities. The results of this analysis are used to set realistic goals and objectives that are aligned with actionable online tactics and to map out an attainable plan for making a real online impact.
- **How do I use a Digital Branch strategic plan?** Compare it to the steps you take when opening a new brick-and-

mortar branch—you explore market trends and growth potentials as well as an operational plan and financial goals. Your Digital Branch plan provides a similar framework to keep your organization focused, secure appropriate stakeholder buy-in, establish how the initiative is resourced, and provide a way to measure success.

Case Study

An industrial parts distributor was on the launch of their second DigitalBranch. While the first webstore was mildly successful, the second one lacked direction—there was no structure, plan, or objectives. As a result, they ended up launching a site that wasn't built for their customers.

The distributor then had to work backwards. Working with B2X Partners, they built a plan created around the X eCommerce System—to put stakes in the ground and define a direction for the future. Using the plan as a guiding tool, the distributor changed direction—addressing technology, operations, and the people involved. They then successfully launched a customer-centric eCommerce site, with the operational and technological foundations for growth.

Takeaway

Without a strategic plan, decisions about eCommerce are often made that address short-term problems, personal preferences, or perceived (rather than researched and defined) business needs. A customer-centric, systems-focused plan ensures that the website is built in alignment with the business's organizational structure and overall goals.

Steps to Building a Strategy

1. **Gather information/begin discovery:**
   a. How is our Digital Branch perceived by customers and our internal team?
   b. How is our Digital Branch performing for customers and our internal team?
   c. Who are our competitors, and what are they doing online?

2. **Identify key issues and challenges:**
   a. What are the biggest business issues?
   b. What are your operational challenges?
   c. What people/teams are hindering change?

3. **Identify core objectives:**
   a. What are we trying to achieve?
   b. What is the strategy to achieve this?
   c. What are the three to five key objectives?

4. **Calculate the impact of meeting those objectives:**
   a. What is our financial model?
      ▪ What are our revenue goals?
      ▪ What are the targets we should set over time?
   b. What are the tools we will use to track success?

5. **Identify action items to achieve core objectives:**
   a. What are the tactics for achieving these objectives?
   b. Who is the person responsible for each objective?
   c. What are our priorities for the action items?

6. **Identify the challenges of getting there:**

    a. What are our internal challenges?

    b. What are our external challenges?

    c. What are our unknowns?

7. **Develop a road map:**

    a. What is our timeline?

    b. What are our milestones?

    c. What resources do we need?

Once you have your plan, this will be your primary tool for driving technology initiatives, marketing planning, and resourcing. This plan will help you start conversations with technology providers and other third-party providers, ensuring that their tools meet your business's objectives.

Your Action Plan

1. Perform your own discovery.
2. Develop your Digital Branch strategic plan.
3. Communicate your plan within your organization.
4. Use your plan as the framework for making major decisions facing the Digital Branch.
5. Like Amazon, write out your plans in an internal press release. Keep refining the messaging as you get feedback and incorporate new ideas.[8]

CHAPTER 4

People
Building Your Digital Team

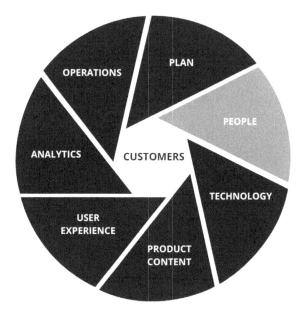

Now you have a new challenge: staffing your Digital Branch. Unlike physical branches you've opened, this branch needs different people with different skills. Also unlike your physical branches, some of this work can be outsourced—even done out of state (or out of the country)—giving you hiring flexibility and a broader pool of candidates.

You need to be serious about putting the right people in the right seats. Your Digital Branch will be a new way of thinking, working, and growing than what may come naturally in your company.

Where can you give existing people new opportunities, which current staff members aren't a good fit, and where are new people needed to achieve the goals in your plan?

Most people assume that great bus drivers (read: business leaders) immediately start the journey by announcing to the people on the bus where they're going—by setting a new direction or by articulating a fresh corporate vision.

In fact, leaders of companies that go from good to great start not with "where" but with "who." They start by getting the right people on the bus, the wrong people off the bus, and the right people in the right seats. And they stick with that discipline—first the people, then the direction—no matter how dire the circumstances.

—Jim Collins, *Good to Great*[9]

Building Your eCommerce Team

As you start defining the seats, here are a few things to keep in mind:

- One person can have multiple seats. Maybe one person can manage product content, Google Analytics, and search engine optimization (SEO).
- The right person can be in the wrong seat. Reconfigure the role so the individual is in the right seat.
- The wrong person can be in the right seat. The seat is right—and the job needs to be done—but the individual is the wrong person to do it.

Start with a Steering Committee

The steering committee is the governance body of your entire Digital Branch. The steering committee is responsible for defining and hiring the people that drive your Digital Branch. This steering committee should include your high-level stakeholders who have input into the following:

- Company values and policies
- Strategic direction of the business
- Budget
- Marketing strategy
- Human resources

At a minimum, the steering committee should include one or two decision makers from leadership, a head of eCommerce (if there is one in place), and an IT leader. For family-owned businesses, this may include family members with a stake or deep personal interest in the business. If building your Digital Branch is a large change to your company culture, this may include internal leaders and influencers, like sales and branch leaders.

Your goal in building a steering committee is twofold:

- To get your team aligned and onboard with the need and value of building an eCommerce team
- To get the right people in the room to vet the best candidates for the positions

If you've assembled the best people within your company and you still don't have a clear vision of how to define the role or vet the right candidates, you may need to bring in a consultant to help this process. This person will sit on your side of the table to articulate your needs and assess the candidates' qualifications. Such consultants will need to demonstrate an understanding of your business goals and company culture. Ideally, if they have been working in this space, they will come with a network of personally known or vouched-for candidates.

Case Study

An HVAC distributor had chosen a head of eCommerce with experience in eCommerce and their ERP. While technically expert, this person wasn't good at communicating with the team. Instead of soliciting and integrating input from the executive leadership, the head of eCommerce dictated the capabilities and the limitations of the site—pushing back on feedback or direction and speaking technical jargon that people didn't understand.

Looking at their business from the X eCommerce System approach, they realized they needed a leader who integrated well with the entire business. Using a job description from B2X Partners, they advertised for, qualified, and hired a new leader. While also a technical and eCommerce expert, the new hire brought an openness to learning about the distribution needs, the specific business needs, individual challenges, and opportunities. A great communicator, the new eCommerce lead was a listener and a teacher—and translated technical jargon into language the executive team and staff could easily understand. This hire was well aligned with the company culture, and as a result, was liked by the executive team and staff.

Takeaway

eCommerce is a technical challenge and requires technical expertise. However, without strong, engaging communication leading it, the business couldn't build an integrated Digital Branch. The Digital Branch leader must be able to learn from, teach, and inspire the executive team and staff. With the X eCommerce System, technology isn't siloed into a separate division; it works in close partnership with business areas in order to create a strong and growing digital business.

Seats That Need to Be Filled

To own your Digital Branch, you need to understand the seats and do a careful, clear-eyed analysis of the team currently and where you need to be. We look at the following seats/skills for a successful eCommerce team.

Use the following chart to help you identify if you have these skills addressed now, if you need to hire someone internally to fill the role, or if you can use a third party to address the skill. Not all roles need to be filled on day one—nor will many businesses be able to start with a fully resourced team—and these roles will continue to expand and grow over time.

SKILL	CURRENT			NOTES
	NOW	HIRE	THIRD PARTY	
Head of eCommerce				Owns the P&L and drives the strategic direction for the eCommerce site, including development, product, marketing, and sales.
Project manager				Acts as the day-to-day contact for all parties. Emphasis on basic eCommerce understanding and good organization skills.
Product content				Responsible for building and maintaining the taxonomy and building the product data, attributes, and images. This person needs to be internal in order to understand how your customers use your content.
Data analyst				Works in Excel, the Product Information Management (PIM), and other data tools to manipulate data, combine data sources, and prepare data to be ready for the website.
Digital marketing				Manages pay-per-click and digital advertising, online promotions, and email marketing.
Social media				Manages the social media accounts, including publishing content on LinkedIn, Facebook, and Twitter. Typically works with digital marketing to develop paid social media strategies.
SEO				Manages how your content and product content is found and optimized on Google and Bing.
Creative/design/ UX				Develops all the creative assets for the site (banners, styles, photos, new pages). Creates wireframes for new pages and processes. Performs user testing and usability studies.
eCommerce Support				Support the internal and customer registration and usage of the site–answering questions, setting up users, and training on how the site works.
Platform analyst				Key role. Learns your major systems (eCommerce, content management system, product information management system, etc.) and executes day-to-day care and feeding, product-content updates, and so on. Less knowledgeable about eCommerce; more of a technical aptitude.
Analytics manager				Performs an ongoing review of site analytics and development of adjustment recommendations.
Developer				Platform developer for eCommerce, CMS, and PIM.

As your business grows in maturity, additional seats will need to be filled:

Developers: Based on your maturity, consider bringing in a few specialty developers:

- Front-end/UX developers
- Back-end developers

Customer Service: Your Digital Branch doesn't eliminate the need for actual humans. You will need dedicated resources on phone, email, and chat to respond to customer inquiries; to manage returns, replacements, and refunds; and to liaise between different operational areas to ensure clear and correct customer communications.

Fulfillment: As the volume of online orders increases, you will need additional support that ensures complete and smooth order fulfillment.

Finance: As your Digital Branch business grows, financial resources will be necessary to understand and address revenue, margin, and loss.

Filling the Right Seat First

Your most important hire is your Digital Branch leader. This will be an endeavor that takes time, effort, and diligence on the part of your business – and where your steering committee can be invaluable. You'll need to find a natural leader who understands your business and aligns with your company culture. This person will be a critical part of your company's future—setting the tone and atmosphere for your eCommerce enterprise. Their success will mean they will build a bigger team underneath them. You want a person who is a great communicator and relationship builder, an evangelist, a good teacher, an avid learner, and a data-driven innovator.

While you undertake this process to find your Digital Branch leader, identify what seats can be filled in the meantime. For example, you may be able to fill product-content resources internally, and digital marketing efforts like email marketing and social media could be done by your existing marketing team.

Sample Organizational Charts

Organizational Chart of a Small Company

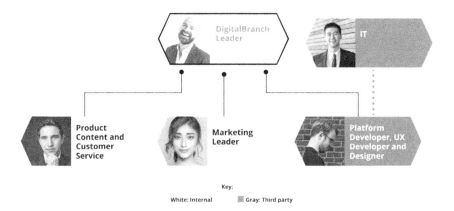

Key:

White: Internal   Gray: Third party

Organizational Chart of a Midsized Company

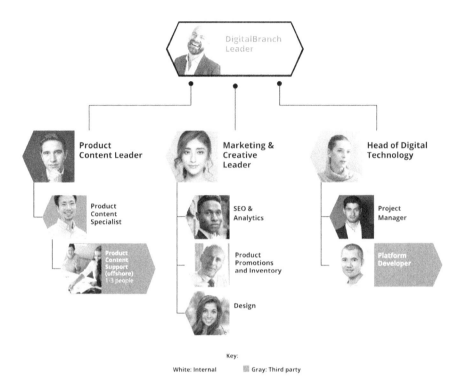

DigitalBranch Leader

Product Content Leader

Product Content Specialist

Product Content Support (offshore) 1-3 people

Marketing & Creative Leader

SEO & Analytics

Product Promotions and Inventory

Design

Head of Digital Technology

Project Manager

Platform Developer

Key:

White: Internal   Gray: Third party

Organizational Chart of a Large Company

DigitalBranch Leader

Product Content Leader

Marketing Leader

Creative Services

Head of Digital Technology

Product Content Analytics

Marketing Programs

Content Writing

Project Manager

Product Content Specialist - Items

Product Promotions and Inventory

Design

Platform Developer

Product Content Support (offshore) 3-4 people

Social Media

UX Design

Website Designer

Product Content Specialist - Maintenance

SEO

Video

Product Content Support (offshore) 1-2 people

Analytics

Key:

White: Internal   Gray: Third party

A third party Product Content Support team can help with:

- Taxonomy
- Attribution
- SKU build
- Attribute gap fill
- Data normalization

Set Clear and Measurable Goals

As you get your team in place, you'll need to ensure they are working together to move the plan forward. For each role, you'll need to set clear and measurable goals. These can be set annually or quarterly but ideally should be made jointly by the person responsible for the goals and the person's manager.

We like SMART goals as a framework. SMART stands for specific, measurable, attainable, relevant, and time-bound goals. This can be done in a simple job scorecard, which is a short list of up to five core goals and up to five measurable actions toward these goals.

Title: **Director of eCommerce**

⚙ Core Responsiblities	📋 End-of-Year Goals
Launch Website	
Relaunch Website	Launch this year
Drive customer registration	10%
Evangelize site internally	1/month trainings
Drive DigitalBranch Revenue	
Online as percent of total revenue	5%
Registrants buying online	25%
Customer repurchase rate	15%
Conversion rate	2%
Drive Product Data	
Find/optimize PIM solution	Launch this year
Optimize data completeness	Increase attribute fill rate to 80%
Launch product merchandising tools	Launch "Customers Who Viewed..." widget
Marketing	
Build Facebook following	5,000
Launch automated email marketing program	Launch this year
Build email list	4,500
Launch advertising campagin	Target ROI: 5:1
Personal Development	
Analytics training	Achieve certification in analytics training
Attend XX conference	Complete this year
Present and launch adoption campaign	Complete this year

In a later chapter, we discuss building the analytics tools to assess your digital business—we call this the scorecard. As you read that chapter, think of how the job scorecard lines up with your business scorecard.

Your Action Plan

1. Complete a clear-eyed audit of your current resources and resource gaps.

2. Create an organizational chart and define how you as an organization will fill those gaps.

3. Prioritize resourcing needs in this recommended order: leadership, product content, customer service, and site management.

4. Build your steering committee and develop job descriptions for seats needed to fill it.

5. Use your plan to qualify and onboard new team members.

CHAPTER 5

Technology
The Tools that Power your Digital Branch

Much like a building is the foundation for your physical branches, your technology systems and software are the foundations for your Digital Branch.

You will need six key technologies to support your Digital Branch:

- eCommerce software
- Content management system (CMS)
- On-site search

- Analytics
- Product information management (PIM)
- Marketing automation

The Role of Your Technology

Your technology (like all components of the XES) should exist to serve your customers. In order of importance, your technology needs to work in two core ways

- provide a great customer experience, making your customers' work life as easy as possible; and
- meet your business objectives and operational needs.

Fundamentally, your customers are going to your site with the expectation that the buying experience will include

- powerful search and simple, intuitive navigation;
- the ability to easily take the next step in the process: transaction (add to cart), quote, request more information, and so on;
- tools to make their job easier: obtain order status, pay invoices, buy using their contract terms and conditions such as pricing and credit; and
- consistent information across all touch points and channels: customer service, web, mobile, sales, and inside sales.

This chapter will cover the different technologies available to meet these expectations.

eCommerce Software

Retail companies are very familiar with eCommerce software and platforms. Business-to-consumer (B2C) companies have been working with eCommerce systems for years—they understand the tools and have the talent to support them. B2C companies understand their business requirements and know the right questions to ask in order to evaluate the different solutions in the marketplace.

Now, here is where the problem arises.

Ask a typical B2B organization, "Do you have the experience to properly evaluate eCommerce software to assess the right fit for your organization?" In our experience, the answer for most businesses will be an emphatic, "No."

If the same B2B company were selecting a new enterprise resource planning system (ERP), a tremendous level of expertise would drive the process. A team of qualified people with the right knowledge would be in place to choose the best platform for the business. In this case, you are not selecting an ERP, so the challenges are unfamiliar as you chart new territory and select a new eCommerce platform.

Dealing with Your Complexity

B2B organizations are complex. This is a result of the dynamics surrounding customers, ordering processes, product mix, and internal systems. Because of this complexity, B2B companies need to build a digital customer experience that includes

- integrating with the backbone of the business: the ERP;
- simplifying complex products and product relationships;
- translating complex customer ordering processes online; and

- extending the sales and service relationships online.

Case Study

An electrical distribution company was trying to decide between two software solutions that were known to work with their ERP. As part of the strategic plan, B2X Partners identified a more detailed list of requirements, created use-cases, and identified a third vendor that could help meet these requirements.

After vendor demonstrations, the distributor decided to go with a third vendor that better met their now fleshed-out requirements and was also a good cultural fit. For this distributor, they preferred to bring in a software company and a separate implementation partner, which gave them the flexibility to change implementation partners in the future. (Some distributors prefer an all-in-one ("one throat to choke") software and implementation partner).

In the end, the company launched with a new website in six months and has a happy relationship with both the software and implementation partners.

Takeaway

To get the best vendor partner, distributors have to deeply understand and define their business requirements and their business culture. A detailed requirements document shared with partners will highlight the core differences in vendors. Launching a site takes a lot of time and effort, so the vendor partner or partners must be people that the company trusts, enjoys working with, and respects (and feels respected by).

ERP Integration

The ERP is the lifeblood for most manufacturers and distributors. B2B companies have to focus a tremendous amount of resources on integrating the ERP to plug into that lifeblood. Think about this:

- Integrating the ERP system(s) will most likely be one of the B2B company's biggest initial and ongoing costs in any B2B eCommerce project.
- Most B2B companies have more than one ERP system because of multiple acquisitions and the time and cost involved in consolidating into a single ERP.
- Many of the B2B features that exist on websites today are about making ERP functions customer-facing.

You will want to have tight integration between your eCommerce system and ERP. Safeguards must be in place—the integration must buffer each system so that if one goes down, the other doesn't necessarily go down. But integration needs to be tight enough to have real-time inventory availability across warehouses, pricing per customer contract, and order status (among other things).

Organization, Contracts, and Pricing

B2B contracts are negotiated between you and your buyer to include

- products that are allowed to be purchased;
- the price at which they are purchased; and
- terms and conditions.

Contracts are part of what make B2B eCommerce difficult to execute. When customers log in, they need to be presented with only what their contract allows them. Search, navigation, and product detail pages should be in sync with the contract to limit the products the customers can view and purchase. The pricing that is displayed on the product detail page should be the contracted price per that product (including volume). This is true even if the price is lower on the "unauthenticated" site, which is the public site—or what can be viewed without logging in.

What makes this even more complex is that a single organization may have multiple contracts applied to different business units or cost centers in the organization. If all of this applies to your business, then you will need a platform that can manage complex organizations.

Taxable/Nontaxable

International and regional tax tables are significantly more complex in B2B.

PunchOut

Many companies use procurement systems or e-procurement solutions to buy their products. Many of your customers may force their employees to purchase through the e-procurement software. In order for those buyers to see your products, the e-procurement software should punchout to your eCommerce site, fill the cart, and then check out in their own e-procurement system. This is also called a round trip.

Other Tools to Manage Your Digital Branch

Beyond your eCommerce platform, there are a number of tools you will need to put in place to manage and grow your DigitalBranch. These tools may be part of the standard features of an eCommerce platform or may require a third-party solution. Even if these features are standard in your eCommerce platform, you may need to look to third-party tools that better fit your business needs and objectives. These tools include:

- Content Management System (CMS)
- On-site Search
- Data Analytics
- Product Information Management (PIM)
- Marketing Automation Platform

Content Management System (CMS)

To manage and leverage your eCommerce site, you need a clearly organized and easy-to-use content management system (CMS). This will allow you to update content, images, and information as well as create new pages, all without technical development intervention.

Your CMS should enable you to manage the following:

- View and edit the Cascading Style Sheets (CSS)
- Create pages
- Edit pages
- Manage images
- Manage videos
- Manage attachments
- Manage content workflow

On-site Search

Sixty percent of B2B buyers listed this as one of their top three features, with 48% of B2B sellers citing enhanced search as a top technology priority

—Accenture Report: "Building the B2B OmniChannel Commerce Platform of the Future"[10]

If you have more than a few hundred SKUs, how do you expect customers to find the product they are looking for? Using navigation by itself takes five to six clicks at best. We have become a search culture—and a culture that expects good search results. B2B is no different. From Amazon to Grainger, the search box is the most used feature. And you know from your own experience how frustrating it is to use a search box and get bad results.

There is a simple way to improve a company's B2B eCommerce site: focus on search. Let me say it in the most straightforward way I can:

Your on-site search sucks. Fix it. It will dramatically improve your customers' experience.

—Justin King

Most people have had a bad search experience at work or at home. The infamous "zero results found" message or a list of irrelevant search results is guaranteed to frustrate even the most patient user. A few minutes or even seconds of that kind of experience is enough. So they leave.

For B2B, on-site search is even more important. A B2B company's products are typically complex with lots of detail, specifications, attributes, and variants. There may be lots and lots of products (hundreds of thousands or even millions). Most B2B users want their search to include the following:

- Context—the search should be personalized by who the user is (industry, company, role)
- Contract—what products they can buy and the agreed-upon price
- Warehouse inventory
- Manufacturer part number
- Competitor cross-reference
- Part-number matching (stripping out special characters)
- Automated spell check
- Past orders—the ability to search and filter based on what the user has purchased in the past

This brings us full-circle to Tim Parry in Multichannel Merchant:

> *When asked to cite the top features or functions they would most like from suppliers in the selling process, most business buyers chose enhanced search functionality on their website (60%).*
>
> **—Tim Parry, Multichannel Merchant**[11]

That's why the best of the B2B eCommerce companies have focused on on-site search.

Note: Good search is based on good data. Make product data and content a priority within your organization. We dive further into this in our **Product Content** chapter—one of the core components of the XES.

Data Analytics Tools

> *If you can't measure it, you can't improve it.*
>
> **—Peter Drucker**, **renowned consultant and author**

Your online business is no different than a brick-and-mortar location in the sense that you need to understand how your Digital Branch generates revenue and how to measure it. One of the many benefits of doing business online is the ability to quantify—in great detail—how your business is doing.

Unlike a brick-and-mortar location, simple technology is readily available to help you easily track your online visitors and their behavior—everything from how many visitors come and how long they stay to what they look at and whether they purchase on their first, second, or third visit, and so on. We will go into further detail in our **Analytics** chapter.

However, to start tracking, you'll need to implement analytics tools. Here are some analytics tools currently available:

- **Google Analytics.** This is a free website-tracking tool that captures detailed website user behavior and website performance through a user-friendly dashboard.
- **PIWIK.** A more robust website analytics software, which does have a cost (unlike Google Analytics) but gives you ownership of your data.

- **Hotjar.** An inexpensive heatmap and user tracking tool that reports on user behavior (click, move, scroll, etc.), records users on your site, presents conversion funnels and form analysis, and provides an integrated survey tool to capture user feedback.

- **Google Tag Manager (GTM).** GTM is a single location that allows you to instantly add other analytics tools (including Facebook Pixel, HotJar, Google Analytics, PIWIK, and others) without the need for coding or development effort.

Online tools like Google Analytics and PIWIK can provide important data on website performance as well as insight into how users engage with your site. To see more customer-specific (or customer group–specific) data such as value per customer or customer retention rates, you'll look to your ERP.

Product Information Management (PIM)

Product data is critical to your success. Product data and content are foundational to SEO, search, navigation, and the overall customer experience. A product information management system (PIM) is software that allows you to easily organize and manage your product data.

eCommerce platforms that focus on product content have rich content-editing features that are closer to what a standalone PIM would provide. In fact, some B2B companies use their eCommerce platforms as their PIM. These platforms provide enough functionality to support standard eCommerce activities for managing the taxonomy and adding descriptions, images, and attributes.

If you do not have a PIM, you should carefully consider the PIM features of an eCommerce platform as well as third-party PIM vendors. Your PIM selection should follow your taxonomy and attribute efforts. We go into further detail on defining your product data needs and structure in our **Product Content** chapter.

Marketing Automation Platform

In order to drive your marketing and communication efforts, you'll need a platform that works with your current systems—especially your eCommerce platform and analytics tools. A marketing platform lets you manage your marketing campaigns with automation that allows you to leverage data to drive preset campaigns. An email marketing platform (like AWeber, ConstantContact, MailChimp, etc.) covers basic marketing automation needs, allowing you to

- set up email marketing campaigns; and
- create automated email funnels for different events, such as
    - a new signup to the website;
    - a new addition to a list; and
    - an action on the site (like a purchase).

More complex marketing automation platforms can also include features like

- online marketing tools (landing pages, A/B testing, forms);
- lead and customer management, with an overview of how customers are interacting with your marketing;
- marketing campaign management;
- planning and scheduling of social media posts, and tracking and "watching" social media for mentions; and

- planning, budgeting, and calendaring tools.

Your Action Plan

1. Define the technology gaps and build a timeline for prioritizing their implementation (recommended order: eCommerce software, analytics, PIM, marketing automation).

2. Build a team to understand the requirements needed to vet new technologies. If you don't have the team, you may need to bring in a third-party consultant to support this process.

3. Understand the differentiators and the real price of implementation.

4. Ensure your team is well trained, well versed in any new products and technologies, and up to date with product development and updates.

CHAPTER 6

Product Content
The Data That Drives Your Customer Experience

Product Content is the data that drives your eCommerce business—it's the information about every product you sell online. Great product data includes detailed, rich, and industry-specific information about the individual products you sell. Having well-structured product content allows you to leverage that data for tools like on-site search, navigation and filtering, and merchandising tools.

Why Product Content Matters

In brick-and-mortar, your shelves have the products displayed and organized, and the salespeople have the product information. Online, though, there are no shelves and no salespeople. The only way customers can experience or understand the product is virtually, based on the functionality of your website. Online, product data is more than just specs—it *is* the product.

Your customers are online. If they aren't buying online, they are researching online—and if they aren't researching, they are making bad buying decisions. Over the next five years, trends indicate traffic will move from "researching only" to "researching and buying." The effectiveness of your site at supporting both functions will determine whether customers continue to buy from you or find a competitor who can serve them better.

The best way for companies to succeed in driving research and sales online is through an effective product content program. High-performing keyword search, highly relevant attribute filtering, and persuasive product detail pages all contribute to B2B eCommerce success. Each of these tools is powered by well-organized product content.

To build this correctly, you need to have a comprehensive strategy for product content, including how it is designed, built, and governed as well as ongoing resources to improve it based on analytics.

A few notes on what product content is not:

- Product content is not a one-time project that can be "fixed." This is a **program**—an ongoing, ever-evolving, and resource-dependent component of your Digital Branch.
- Product content is not a cost center that must be minimized at all costs. Rather, it is an **asset** and needs to be measured and accounted for as any other asset is.

- Product content is **not static**. As your selection evolves, your content needs to stay current—processes must be in place to watch for changes and ensure ongoing compliance with the strategy.

When managed strategically, product content becomes more than a nuisance—it becomes a sustainable source of competitive advantage that drives revenue, profits, and customer satisfaction. In this section, we discuss our approach to product content and why each step matters. From there on, it's up to you.

How to Organize Product Content

A reason that B2B eCommerce sites fail is bad product content – product content that is disorganized, inconsistent, or incomplete. Unlike B2C sites, where products often sell based on popularity and trends, sales of B2B products are primarily based on whether the item is effective for a given application. Determining whether a product fits an application requires complete, clear, and consistent product content not only to find the right *type* of product but also to differentiate each individual item within that category from others. Also, it's critical to clearly show *why* the product works. For product content to do this successfully, it must be highly structured.

In the context of product content, "structured" means the content is made to exact standards and guidelines—following a "rulebook," that defines what information is required for each product sold. In eCommerce, websites rely on a virtual organizational structure called a data model. Data models consist of two components that document the structure needed for B2B content:

Taxonomies are hierarchical grouping methodologies that group things with other similar things. Usually seen in the "left-hand browse" list of product categories, taxonomies are analogous to a brick-and-mortar store layout. Just as brick-and-mortar stores put similar items near each other to make it easier for buyers to compare, effective taxonomies place similar products near each other in the product hierarchy. Well-structured taxonomies facilitate product discovery but also impact SEO, marketing, and data governance, so they are a critical foundation for eCommerce success.

Attributes describe the features of a product that buyers use to differentiate products within each category of the taxonomy. Once they have found the right product category for their application, buyers use those features to select a specific product. Using attributes to pick products in eCommerce is similar to brick-and-mortar buying.

In a brick-and-mortar store, buyers can hold the items in their hands and compare them side by side. Brick-and-mortar stores don't have to account for each attribute individually because they are obvious to the buyer (e.g., weight, color, size, material). But in eCommerce, the attributes (and their associated values) can only be compared if they are explicit and shown on the product detail page. To that end, effective attribution includes identifying, documenting, and defining all attributes that describe the features that are used (or could be used) for comparison.

Different types of attributes capture different aspects of each product. Each type can serve different purposes in eCommerce, but all are frequently used. The three primary features captured as attributes are

- descriptive qualities (e.g., material, shape, color, special features);
- performance qualities (application, speed, voltage); and
- relationship qualities (compatible materials, compatible products, accessory products).

Each category of product that you sell requires a complete accounting of all attributes. This ensures that customers can easily identify the best item for their application and prevents product duplication within the category. To document the attribute requirements for a site, the following information must be defined for each category:

- Attribute name—what the attribute will be called in the design (if there are multiple terms for the same product type, choose one as the primary)
- Attribute type—number, integer, text, LOV (values limited to a constrained set), Boolean
- Whether the attribute can be multivalued (e.g., a "compatible materials" attribute could have two values of "steel" and "aluminum")
- A list of values that each attribute can have (either a set of representative examples or the full list, if limited)
- Whether the attributes should be used for faceted search (and in what order they should be displayed)
- An easy-to-understand definition for the attribute
- The order in which attributes are displayed on a product detail page
- Whether the attribute is required to be populated for all items in the category

How Structured Product Content Serves Customers (and You)

Taxonomies and attributes provide the foundation for digital commerce, driving product discovery and conversion. Structured content provides the guidelines needed to use the content effectively. But simply having a data model in place is not enough on its own—the content for each item has to comply with the structure captured in the data model. What's more, the content has to meet the "three Cs" of product content—it must be clear, complete, and consistent.

- **Clear**: The values of the attributes should avoid technical or confusing terminology such as trade jargon and obscure abbreviations, which limit buyers' ability to recognize the features.

- **Complete**: If an attribute is required for a given product type, then all SKUs of that type should have a value for that attribute populated; failure to do so means buyers using that attribute will miss any SKUs without that attribute.

- **Consistent**: The values for a given attribute used to describe a specific product type are formatted consistently, (e.g., "1 inch" instead of "1 inches," "1.00 inch," or "1 in.") and use consistent terminology across all items.

Even if the attribute data of a product complies with your data model, violating the "three Cs" can still hinder your success. The "three Cs" provide a way to ensure that the structure of the data model is still relevant for humans. That helps companies experiment with design, user interface (UI) tools, and marketing that is build on a shared universal set of structured data.

This is where you want to take a customer-centric approach to defining your taxonomy as well as your attributes. When evaluating your content, be sure to include people who can speak to actual customer needs and wants. This is a great way to draw from the expertise of your sales team and customer and product experts to define what this means for your business and ensure that your data model stays customer focused.

Product Data Sources

With a robust data model in place, the next step is to determine where you will obtain the product content to populate it. This is an often overlooked pain point for B2B and can be a challenge to manage. Failure to be strategic about sourcing often results in content that ranges from partially flawed to completely broken. In either case, the effort needed to recover and "fix" the problems usually ends up being more expensive than the initial build.

With that in mind, you have options. There are a number of approaches to sourcing product data, each of which comes with its own advantages and disadvantages.

Manufacturer Sourcing

Obtaining product data from the manufacturers that supply the product is a preferred option, because manufacturers usually have the most complete sets of product content. Also, in cases where content is missing, they are best positioned to add it. Moreover, manufacturers may be able to create a custom export of their data that better matches your needs, reducing reworking needed to meet the requirements of your data model.

However, manufacturers have limited capacity to respond to requests for data, so depending on your relationship, they may not be able (or willing) to help you. In some cases, manufacturers might provide a standard export, but that may need additional manipulation or formatting before importing.

Pros

- Represents an authoritative data source
- (Usually) provides indemnification coverage
- (Typically) ensures consistent data

Cons

- Requires good partnership
- Is incremental—one manufacturer at a time
- Can be hard to scale as supplier count increases

In-House Content Team

The alternative to manufacturer sourcing is to build everything using internal resources. This approach ranges from deploying a team of full-time staff to find attribute data from supplier websites, write copy, take images, and so on down to having the owner's kid work part-time as an intern during breaks from school. This approach usually returns very high-quality results but is typically difficult to scale up as the business grows and can be expensive to staff—both in terms of cost and effort needed to recruit and hire.

Pros

- Offers good control over data model compliance
- Ensures consistent data
- Provides strong differentiation

Cons

- Is difficult to scale as SKU count grows
- Entails staffing costs
- Requires recruiting effort

Offshore Partner Sourcing

In recent years there has been significant growth in the launch of offshore firms that provide product-data sourcing services to firms in the B2B space. That said, not all offshore service providers have experience with the kinds of product carried by B2B firms, so it is critical to assess their experience or capabilities before moving forward. If you have a strong data model, you may be able to use a less experienced firm, but that is no guarantee. Regardless, be sure to request references from current clients and—whenever possible—request a sample of data to evaluate how well the service provider can deliver SKU data that complies with your data model before fully engaging.

Pros

- Is scalable
- Is cost effective
- Can flex capacity to meet requirements

Cons

- May be harder to manage due to distance
- May lack experience with your product categories
- Requires robust and complete data model (with metadata) for successful compliance

Third Party Data Pools

Some firms or industry associations have started services with which they compile sets of SKU data across multiple brands, manufacturers, and suppliers. By pooling SKU data, these companies offer access to large volumes of SKU data that would otherwise be expensive and time consuming to produce independently. While these options are frequently less expensive than the other options discussed above, they may have built out large libraries of SKUs by setting low standards for product data quality, requiring additional work to normalize/standardize the data.

Pros

- Is scalable
- Is inexpensive
- Typically provides automated updates

Cons

- Offers limited control over values
- Data quality may be poor
- May pose difficulties in complying with data models

Third-Party Data Pools

Some firms and industry associations have services that compile sets of SKU data across multiple brands, manufacturers, and suppliers. By pooling SKU data, these companies offer access to large volumes of SKU data that would otherwise be expensive and time consuming to produce independently. While these options are frequently less expensive than the other options discussed above, they may have built out large libraries of SKUs by setting low standards for product data quality, requiring additional work to normalize/standardize the data.

Pros

- Is scalable
- Is inexpensive
- Typically provides automated updates

Cons

- Offers limited control over values
- Data quality may be poor
- May pose difficulties in complying with data models

Here are a few questions to help you evaluate a product content source:

- Where will your product data come from (from the manufacturer, from a third-party seller, from a subscription service, or from a combination of multiple sources)?

- How well does the data from this source match up with the structure established in your data model? Does it have good fill rates for attributes (particularly those you are targeting for faceted search)? Are attribute values normalized across brands or manufacturers?

- What rich-media assets does this source provide for your most important products? Does it include clear images, detailed descriptions, CAD files, MSDSs, and videos?

- How customizable is the formatting of the content from the source? Can you customize what attributes are sent? Can you limit it only to a list of SKUs you provide?

- How will you fill gaps in product data? What resources do you need to provide to make the data from the source meet your requirements?

Case Study

With our background in product content software and product optimization especially in the distribution industries, B2X Partners was brought in to help a large buying group create a product data aggregation service for their members. To serve their members, we helped architect an industry-focused platform with a full taxonomy and content program. B2X Partners helped the selection and procurement of product content vendors to build a product content program with millions of SKUs and thousands of attributes. B2X Partners also worked with individual distributors to take and adopt that taxonomy and content to best meet their specific industry and customer needs.

Takeaway

Product content is a challenge—and a broadly built taxonomy will likely not serve your customers or your website. Product taxonomy is the foundation, and product content is the data that drives the user experience on your website. Defining this as specifically as you can for your business and your customers is critical to helping your customers research and discover your products online.

Optimizing Product Content

With your data model complete and your SKU data built in compliance with the data model, the heavy lifting of the initial setup of your product selection is complete. However, your work has just begun! A content-focused approach to eCommerce requires more than just the initial build—it also needs a plan to support, maintain, and improve your content over time.

Once the first version has been created, it's critical to make sure that the SKU data remains in compliance with the data model. This is called data governance. Data governance can take many forms depending on the capabilities of the tools used. It can be anything from using native Excel features (filters, pivot tables, slicers, or conditional formatting), to customized SQL queries applied to the item database itself, to automated defect detection as part of native data-governance capabilities within a PIM.

In all cases, the intent behind data governance is to automate— however possible—the detection of SKUs that have changed or were created in such a way that they are no longer compliant with the data model. Data governance that is not automated usually fails over time due to the sheer volume of potential errors. Other approaches to data quality, such as workflows and manual approvals, cannot scale to the degree required, and firms using this approach often see their content quality degrade in only a few years, losing the value of their initial investment as well as their ability to differentiate themselves from competitors.

With data governance in place, the next step is to leverage web analytics data to observe how customers interact with your data model as presented on your site. The impact of product content on the user experience is significant, and you should make sure that your analytics package is able to help you evaluate the effectiveness of every component of your content asset. Consider the following examples:

- **Taxonomy:** Are customers able to browse your taxonomy easily? Are there particular categories that are underperforming compared to other categories located nearby in the hierarchy?

- **Attributes:** Are there additional attributes you should use as faceted search for a particular category? Are new attributes needed to differentiate new selections being added?

- **Data source:** As traffic or revenues grow in a category, should you consider using higher-quality data sources to improve compliance, boost fill rates, or improve consistency?

- **User experience:** Are there categories that feature faceted search where users are not successfully finding products? Are they even engaging with the faceted search options offered? Do you need to consider enabling additional attributes as faceted search? Would adding educational content to the landing page help customers be more decisive?

- **Data governance:** Are your data-governance rules still current with the changes you have made to the data model? Do opportunities exist to better automate defect detection?

- **Rich-media assets:** Do products exist that are underperforming in terms of conversion where additional images, video, CAD files, PDFs of literature could be added to the detail page to give customers more confidence to buy?

- **Merchandising strategy:** Are there ways to better present products as complete solutions rather than single SKUs? Can you highlight related products (e.g., accessories, substituted/upgraded SKUs, configurators to build assemblies or systems, and compatibility checkers) using the improved content in your content asset?

Your Action Plan

1. Understand the current state of your product data.

2. Define a product taxonomy and attribute structure that supports the kind of user experience you intend for your customers.

3. Define the technology needs—either within your current or future eCommerce platform or an external PIM.

4. Develop a product-data sourcing strategy to get your SKU data up to the baseline of your data model.

5. Establish a data-governance program to keep your asset at a high level of quality and to start the drive for automation.

6. Integrate web analytics with your content program to identify ways to raise the bar on customer experience and stay ahead of the competition at creating a site that delights your users.

7. Iterate all the above repeatedly over time, matching your customer trends and patterns with investments targeted at improved content, and measuring results using A/B testing and user analytics.

CHAPTER 7

User Experience
Creating a Customer-Centric Digital Branch

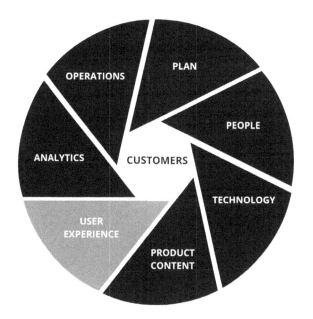

At B2X, we look at user experience and design **early and often** when building the Digital Branch. This means planning and designing a consistent look and feel throughout all touch points both in visual design (branding, color, fonts) and user experience (user flows, ease of use, interaction patterns, etc.). It also includes building in a process and system for researching, testing, and learning how users engage with your site.

What Is Customer-Centric Design?

Is your website designed with your business or your customers in mind? Have you considered every touch point with customers throughout their online and offline experience—from search and product research through checkout process to actual product delivery? Customer-centric design means

1. understanding your customers' motivations and needs; and

2. creating and adapting your Digital Branch design to meet those needs.

Customer-Centric Design and B2B eCommerce

Customer-centric design approaches can be seen across nearly all industries, from B2C retail eCommerce sites to government agencies.

In the B2B eCommerce landscape, customer centricity can be a differentiator for customers who need a seamless and simple online experience. Because B2B customers are visiting your eCommerce site out of necessity rather than leisure, they have specific and often complex needs. Your goal is to understand the motivations, challenges, and behaviors of these customers and to design an online experience to meet their unique needs. By understanding this, you can design your site to be intuitive, clear, and rewarding, helping you increase conversions and build long-lasting customer and business relationships.

Customer Centric Design: Where Customer and Business Goals Converge

So, what makes B2B eCommerce customers unique, and how do you design to meet their needs? While the specific requirements will vary by industry and company, generally B2B customer-centric design means focusing on helping your customers get their jobs done as quickly and easily as possible. At the highest level, your customers have very basic goals when they reach your website:

- I need to purchase a specific product.
- I need to research products (for later purchase).
- I need to manage my account.

What these three high-level goals mean and how they should influence design decisions varies depending on the specific company goals.

Case Study

An industrial distributor was launching its first true eCommerce site. Their software implementer was leading the user experience and design—but this vendor didn't have experience with their industry or customers. B2X Partners stepped in to define and design a user experience that was focused on their customers.

Using customer interviews, analytics, user testing, and industry best practices, B2X designed a site to meet their customer's needs, making it faster and easier to do their job. The design focused on search, product information, easy registration and checkout, and a streamlined, simplified experience.

Beyond that, B2X designed a separate experience for registered customers. After logging in, the website experience changed, to work more like an application than a website. The distributor's branding disappeared and was replaced by their customer's logo and profile. The customer's most needed tools, like quick order, order history, and recent products, were put front and center on an easy to access dashboard.

Takeaway

While design doesn't look complex, designing a site that serves your customer has to be guided by knowing your business goals and knowing what your customers want to achieve on your site. By understanding the value your customers place on items like quick order versus recently viewed products, for example, you can design the site so that the most important, useful, and actionable information gets the best real estate on your site.

How to Get Started

Start with your customers and work backward.

—Jeff Bezos[12]

User research is the foundation of a customer-first approach. Without a clear understanding of the challenges your customers face in their daily work life, your eCommerce site may fail to solve their real problems. There are many ways to learn more about your customers and how they interact with your site—and, often more importantly, why they behave the way they do.

- **Surveys.** Surveys can be done by canvassing your current customers, surveying like-minded buyers, and conducting on-site surveys (usually one to three questions) that capture immediate feedback. Many tools are available for on-site surveys, including Hotjar.

- **A/B and multivariate testing.** Multivariate testing is a way to see how your audience responds to different prompts. On websites, it is used to test what colors, copy, images, and placement attract more engagement. It can also be used for content marketing on email and social media to see what language and messages resonate most with your audience.

- **Analytics.** By understanding and assessing your analytics data, you can use this quantitative data to drive design decisions. We go deeper into your analytics in a later chapter.

- **Customer interviews and focus groups.** Soliciting feedback from individual customers or a group of customers can help you gather valuable information on what they actually need and expect from your Digital Branch. It may be different than what you assume.

As you gather this information, know that another powerful tool exists to help you understand user expectations and shape your site experience to meet these. It is a process we call customer experience journey mapping.

Customer Experience Journey Mapping

Journey mapping is a technique to help you better understand how your customers interact with your business at every touch point. It involves a few core exercises:

- Defining user personas—three to five composites of your core users
- Mapping how your customers interact with your business
- Understanding the touch points—where your customers experience your business

By articulating the **personas of your customers** and the **touch points they encounter**, you can start optimizing your user experience to best meet their needs.

What Is Customer Experience Journey Mapping?

A customer journey map is a visual roadmap of your customers' buying experiences from their perspective—including their highs and lows and their points of direct contact with your company (touch points). The journey map shows your customers' frontline interactions with company reps as well as behind-the-scenes support services and how well they serve your customers' needs. Your goal is to build a visual guide to your key customers' paths through your company's buying cycle, identifying pain points, solutions, and KPIs.

The Value of Journey Mapping

As we quoted at the beginning of this book, your customers are simple; it's your business that is complicated. As your customers engage with your Digital Branch, it needs to look and feel like your brick-and-mortar branches. The digital experience should be seamless—from research and purchase to returns and replacements.

As you gain understanding of the touch points (your branches, your website, your social media, your sales team), you can identify the opportunities and challenges to delivering a consistent message. As you map out the complexities of your customers' interactions with your business (it may be seven different people who make sure an order is right), you'll understand the dependencies and complexities of delivering a unified experience.

Research has shown that positive customer experience is a game changer:[15]

- Gartner Group says that 89 percent of companies compete on customer experience.
- However, only 11 percent of companies use customer data to make decisions affecting customers.
- Customer-centric companies enjoy 55 percent greater customer retention rates.
- Better customer experience yields an average year-over-year 23 percent decrease in customer service costs.

Implementing Journey Mapping

Customer journey mapping is an effort requiring dedicated time and resources. We recommend doing this before site redesigns or site relaunches, major campaigns, or new initiatives. Here's what you'll need:

- **Step 1:** Get leadership sponsorship for your effort. This needs to be spearheaded or sponsored by someone who understands the value and the importance of the exercise and who can dedicate resources to it.

- **Step 2:** Conduct research and make observations—use the research tools outlined earlier in this chapter to start building
  - user personas;
  - a general customer pathway;
  - pain points; and
  - KPIs—the metrics you will use to measure performance and change.

- **Step 3:** Schedule sessions with key team members impacting user experience. These people may include customer service, marketing, warehouse, operations, and finance representatives.

- **Step 4:** In these sessions, walk through the customer personas and the user pathways. Identify and problem-solve around pain points, obstacles, and issues. Identify and clarify KPIs.

- **Step 5:** After the sessions, follow up with a clear roadmap of priorities and KPIs to change. Use this document to drive design, technology, and marketing decisions moving forward.

User Experience and Design

Your design is where your site "comes to life." It is the visual interpretation of your plan, your technology, and your focus on building a customer-centric tool. You don't need to be an artist to assess whether your site design is helping you achieve these goals. Your site designs should be intentional and follow best practices for user interface (UI) design and interaction patterns. Ask your design team why they made certain design decisions, and make sure their intentions match your goals. Don't let jargon or trends get in the way of your business plan.

Your Digital Branch isn't simply a work of art. It needs to be a combination of form and function. Beautifully rendered designs can fail if customers still can't do what they need to do. You need to consider both aesthetics and functionality when designing your site.

We have developed a few B2B design best practices that we adhere to for every client product. These guidelines and directions will ensure the site is easy to use, consistent, and adherent to research in B2B user behavior:

- **Header and navigation:** Design a header and main navigation with a clear hierarchy that focuses on easily finding products.

- **Product categories**: Allow users to find the products they're looking for as quickly as possible. Show them your entire product line in a clear, concise way as soon as they get to your site.

- **On-site search:** Make the on-site search box very visible for users, as most will attempt to search for their product via the search box immediately. Optimize search so that it pushes relevant results as soon as possible to the user to reduce the number of clicks it takes them to find what they're looking for.

- **Product navigation:** Design a product navigation that makes it easy for users to navigate to products using a strong product-category drop-down menu no matter where they are on the site. Display subcategories above the fold—in the area of the website you can see as soon as you open a page, without scrolling down the page.

- **Overall design:** Create a site with clean lines and complementary colors that visually displays prominent elements appropriately and conveys the look and feel of your brand.

Sample Wireframe: Homepage

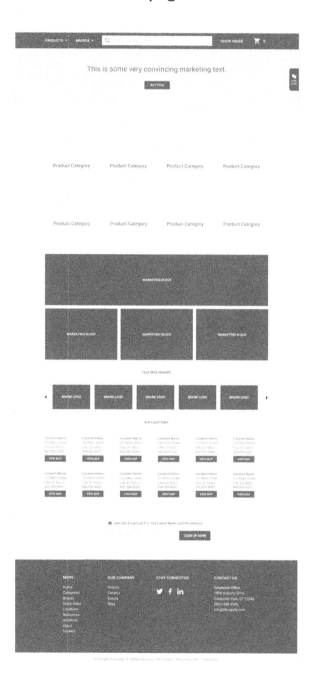

Sample Wireframe: Product Detail Page

Sample Wireframe: My Account

User Experience Testing

After creating the design, you'll want to test to see if your ideas translate into a smooth customer experience. Your design may be visually amazing, but if your customers can't easily shop and check out, then your site will ultimately not be valuable to them.

The best way to ensure that customers will be able to use your site is by conducting user experience (UX) testing throughout the project lifecycle as well as after the launch.

Don't assume. Validate.

—B2X Partners UX Team

While you and your team may think your design is intuitive, you are not your users. The best way to find out if a design works is to watch your customers use it. Testing with even five people can uncover 85 percent of usability issues on a site (Nielson Norman Group).[16]

What to Test?

There are three general types of user testing:

- Discoverability—do users know this feature exists?
- Findability—can users find key services and products?
- Usability—can users use this tool easily?

While your site has a lot of complexity and functionality, your customers are coming for three main purposes: researching products, purchasing products, and managing their accounts. There are many features and workflows that you could test with users, but here are three that will be essential to your site's success:

1. **Product Search**

   Can your users easily find key products by going through your navigation, filtering through categories or through on-site search? Test the following:

   - Find key products through navigation and filtering.

   - Perform an on-site search by common product name.

   - Perform an on-site search by product number.

2. **Checkout Process**

   A streamlined checkout experience is key to converting potential customers. Test the following activities:

   - Select "pay on account" and enter purchase order number.

   - Check out and elect to pick up the order from a specific branch.

   - Update the quantity of an item in the cart.

3. **Product Detail Page**

   Customers are on your site for products, and they need to know specific information to make purchasing decisions. Testing the design of your product detail page can ensure that customers can find essential information about a product. Test the following activities:

   - Find a certain specification for a product.

   - Add a product to a new product list.

   - Find out if this product is available at your local branch.

4. Registration

Most B2B sites require users to have an account to complete purchases, so a simple registration process is vital. If you are allowing both B2B and B2C customers to purchase, your registration process needs to be especially clear. Test the following possible task goals:

- Register as new B2C customer.
- Register as an existing customer.
- Find your account number.

When to Test

You don't need to wait for the site to go live in order to test. Test early and often and make testing a part of the UX and design process. You can test wireframes and early designs as well as final designs for overall usability. As the designs are implemented, you can test more specific features.

The important thing is that you continue to test with users throughout the project and beyond the go-live date. Site launch is only the beginning. When your site is live, you can look for trends in analytics that may be indicative of usability issues and then target those specific areas for a usability test.

How to Test

The testing method and type you select will depend on the goal of the test and the resources available.

Test Method: Quantitative versus Qualitative
Both quantitative and qualitative methods can be used to assess the usability of a site.

- **Qualitative methods** involve observing user behaviors and are best used to answer questions related to behavior, preferences, and perceptions. You don't need to have a working product to perform qualitative testing. Test groups for these types of tests are small (about five participants).

- **Quantitative methods** measure performance and are best used if you need definitive numbers to calculate return on investment, for example. Quantitative studies require a large participant sampling (eighty to thousands of users) and require a functioning site. Thus, these studies are usually done to evaluate the usability of your current site or to define how effective your redesign was by comparing results once the redesigned site is live.

Test Location: On-Site or Lab versus Remote

- **On-site or lab:** If you are doing qualitative research, you have the option to perform tests in person either at your office or the user's home or office or at a usability lab if you have access to one. Testing in-house can be logistically intensive but will also allow more of your team members to observe the tests. Going to a user's site can be especially beneficial to provide context to your studies. Ideally, users would be completing your test tasks in the same environment in which they would normally access your site, so you will get a firsthand look at the external factors that could impact how they use your site. You can also work with a usability lab that will help run the tests with you. Such a facility will also monitor and record (through software on the computers used and/or video recording) what users are doing on your site.

- **Remote (moderated or unmoderated):**
    - **Moderated testing** requires that you have a facilitator who directs the test through some kind of technology. The facilitator observes users as they complete the directed task and has the opportunity to ask follow-up questions. No specific technology is needed—you can use an online meeting tool like GoToMeeting or Zoom to complete a moderated test.
    - With **unmoderated testing**, a panel of user participants accepts your test via a remote testing service (for example, UserTesting, UserZoom, Usabilla) and then reads through and attempts each of the tasks. The service records the session and provides the recordings and results back to you through its website. Unmoderated testing can be a less expensive option but will not allow you to ask follow-up questions or change tasks on the fly.

Start Testing Now

Your Digital Branch is ever evolving, and you should plan to continue to learn more about your customers and how they use your site before and after launch. Flaws can emerge even in the best designs when put in front of real users. Keep these things in mind when starting to test your site:

- Don't assume. Validate.
- Test early and often.

- Use qualitative test methods early in the design to learn about user perceptions and challenges. Use quantitative methods to "prove" your final designs.

- Remember: you are not your users. Let them help you make your site better!

Your Action Plan

1. Research what your customers need from an online experience with your company.

2. If resources and time are available, do a journey-mapping exercise. This is an in-depth, resource-heavy project. You may need to bring in outside help to support this.

3. Focus your design efforts on serving your customers. Whether doing the work with an internal team or an external party, make sure to communicate your strategic plan as well as brand and visual guidelines (like your logo, a style guide, and past marketing materials) so that designers can execute against your goals.

4. Plan on testing before and after launch to continue to learn how well your site serves your customers.

CHAPTER 8

Analytics
Know Your Numbers to Know Your Business

Most B2B companies are flying blindly with no data to tell them where they are and where they are going. Data enables you to monitor your Digital Branch accurately so that you can take effective action and make enhancements to increase the bottom line. Data gives you concrete answers and guidance, enabling you to stop managing by assumptions, subjective opinions, emotions, and egos. It gives you information on how your customers are interacting with you online.

While the massive amount of data collected from selling online on numerous platforms can certainly create a challenge, moving forward, it is one that online merchants will need to handle effectively. Learning to translate that data into actionable information for driving future customer engagement could prove to be a significant asset.

—Brett Relander, founder of Launch & Hustle, LLC[13]

In this chapter, we'll cover two key analytics tools:

- The Executive Scorecard—a macro-level view of how your business is performing
- The Digital Branch Team Scorecard—a more detailed view of how the Digital Branch is performing and of opportunities for action

Where to Start

Your scorecard is specific to your business. The numbers should be driven by the financial model and revenue goals articulated in your plan. While you can Google "eCommerce conversion rate," the number you'll see won't be relevant to your business. The number in your scorecard will be based on where you are today and the actions you are taking today and tomorrow to move that number.

Where the Data Comes From

As we wrote in the **Technology** chapter, how you intend to capture data needs to be included in your technology efforts. In order to assess how your business is performing, you will need to pull data from the following sources:

- Google Analytics or PIWIK
- Your ERP
- HotJar
- Marketing tools/platform (email, social media, etc.)
- Customer service
- Qualitative sources (e.g., customer feedback)
- A/B Testing

Case Study

In order to help a plumbing distributor reach their revenue goals, B2X Partners created an analytics structure that broke down each step toward these goals. This included the adoption framework, as well as KPIs for each step. This effort including getting the entire executive team on board, providing them with the same language to use and questions to ask.

Using Google Analytics and Hotjar, they saw on a macro level how people were performing on their site. They adopted the site design and language to help users navigate areas where they got stuck or left. Through internal communications and incentives, they drove their team to work together to drive their eCommerce business. As a result, they've steadily increased their eCommerce revenue.

Takeaway

While technology supports analytics, the real effort in analytics is in defining and communicating the goals throughout the organization. Creating a common language, clarity in the data, and focused, attainable goals helps the entire organization move toward growing eCommerce as a percentage of revenue.

The Executive Scorecard

Scorecards aren't new. They are ways of highlighting the most important metrics for measuring how your business is performing. And they aren't the only game in town. There are also dashboards—like the one you can see in Google Analytics. It shows the latest feed of data. We like scorecards because they are simple and action focused.

> *Process improvement programs are like teaching people how to fish. Strategy maps and scorecards teach people where to fish.*

> **—Robert S. Kaplan, co-creator and writer of *The Balanced Scorecard*[14]**

The Digital Branch Executive Scorecard is designed to be a quick read—a document that any executive can scan in a minute or two and obtain a clear, forward-moving recommendation that keeps the business on track and moving in the right direction.

The Digital Branch Executive Scorecard is a tool that

- is easy to create in Excel or Google docs;
- is easy to update;
- offers a benchmark of expectations; and
- quickly highlights what is going well and what isn't.

Here's an example of a clean and straightforward **Executive Scorecard:**

	Owner	Goal (Week)	Week 1	Week 2	Week 3
Revenue					
Total Revenue	Sales	$50,000	$45,000	$51,000	$60,000
eCommerce Revenue	eCommerce	$2,500	$2,400	$2,550	$3,000
eCommerce as a Percent of Revenue	eCommerce	5%	3%	4%	5%
eCommerce Shipping Revenue	eCommerce	$500	$450	$500	$515
Adoption Funnel					
Registered Customers	Sales	10	15	8	12
Logins	eCommerce	200	201	250	190
Orders	eCommerce	100	90	150	105
# of Ordering Customers	eCommerce	75	80	81	90
Conversion Rate	eCommerce	3%	2.5%	2.0%	3.5%
First Orders	eCommerce	5	5	4	3
# of Repeat Orders	eCommerce	50	50	45	30
Average Order Value	eCommerce	$1,200	$1,001	900	$1,250
Abandoned Carts	eCommerce	25	30	35	15
Finance & Operations					
Product Gross Profit	Finance	$27,000	$24,750	$28,050	$33,000
Shipping Gross Profit	Finance	$125	$(500)	$90	$145
Product Cost of Goods	Finance	$22,500	$20,250	$22,950	$27,000
Shipping Cost of Goods	Finance	$300	$400	$300	$275
Shipping Time	Operations	3 Days	3	4	4
Cash Days	Finance	15	20	25	14
Total Operating Expenses	Finance	$20,000	$19,000	$25,000	$27,000
Overall Score (10 for above goal)			80	80	140

Key: ▨ Gray: below target   ■ Black: at or above target

Building this for your business will help build transparency, clarity, and responsibility throughout the company. It's a common tool that all key eCommerce members can reference and drive toward. It helps keep people on track and accountable. The weights assigned to each goal (in the example above, every line above the goal is allocated a score of ten points) are then added in the final line. This provides a very high-level look at performance—as you can see in the score trend graph below.

We recommend looking at your numbers in a twelve-month run rate, paying specific attention to

- the month, year over year;
- the previous month;

- the previous quarter; and
- the trends.

Sample Score:

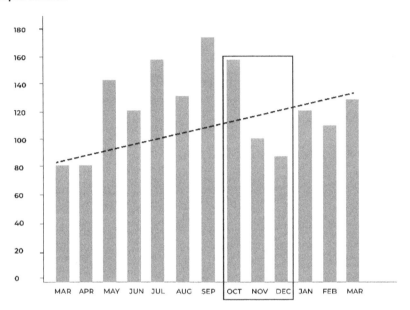

Scorecards should be used weekly to track performance against objectives, thereby reducing surprises and misunderstandings. Each line of the scorecard should be "owned" by one person—the one who is accountable for updating and understanding the number (and the levers to change it). These scorecards are used in leadership meetings to provide executives with a high-level understanding of the Digital Branch's performance.

The Digital Branch Team Scorecard

The Digital Branch team requires a much more detailed view of the digital business. Team members need to understand and own the levers for change. In order to build a scorecard that is action focused, we recommend the following five steps:

1. Establish and communicate measurable goals.
2. Define key performance indicators (KPIs) based on measurable goals.
3. Develop the scorecard.
4. Report regularly.
5. Align budget and marketing to successful KPIs.

Step 1: Establish and Communicate Measurable Goals

Your measurable goals should derive from your plan—which includes a financial model and revenue goals. In order to create useful and relevant goals, you need to start by building a framework for digital success.

The Customer Adoption Framework

The customer adoption framework is a B2B eCommerce strategy framework and a key part of the Digital Branch. The primary question we are answering in this framework is: "How can we get customers to use and adopt our new site?" This framework is based on getting your current customers to use your new eCommerce site as a research and ordering platform.

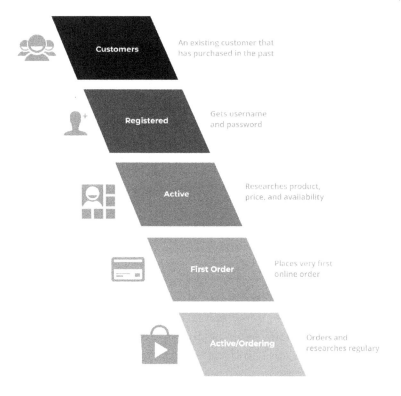

For example, our customer adoption framework looks at the path your customers take to move from nondigital customers to active, ordering, online customers. Based on your knowledge of your customers and your business, what levers can you pull to get the results you want?

The Customer Acquisition Framework

The customer acquisition model is a function of

- traffic;
- conversion; and
- average order value (AOV).

The relevant formula is

$$\text{Revenue} = \text{Traffic} \times \text{Conversion} \times \text{AOV}$$

Acquisition should be focused not just on the transaction but on lead generation. Lead generation is all about content marketing, social media, and SEO.

Step 2: Define Key Performance Indicators (KPIs) Based on Measurable Goals

The term key performance indicators (KPIs) is used to identify data points gathered over time that reflect the performance of your business. While there are many standard KPIs, the ones you track and review in depth will be determined by your business objectives, company values, and management needs. KPIs essentially serve as guideposts in your online channel, highlighting where and how you're meeting (or not meeting) revenue goals and business objectives.

There are many different types of KPIs related to website traffic, registration, website activity, orders, cart, retention, and so on. For B2B activity, however, we recommend focusing on the following:

- Number of customer registrations
- Number of customer logins
- Number of customer page views
- Number of orders
- Average order value (AOV)
- Lines per order
- Campaign start/end
- Referral source

- Source keywords
- Number of orders by product
- Number of orders by product category
- Number of abandoned carts
- Navigation paths to purchase

Below is an example of several different objectives and KPIs that can help measure performance against those objectives:

Sample Objective-Driven Action and KPIs Structure

OBJECTIVE	OBJECTIVE	KPIs
Get customers to register online	Email marketing to customers	Email open rate, Email click rate
Get customers to become active online	Provide guided search	Time on site, Bounce rate
Get active customers to order online	Product merchandising, ensure the perfect order	Average Order Value (AOV), Value per customer

Ultimately, you can use your KPIs to test out ideas and campaigns. For example, you can assess specific web-page performance by looking at measures such as **percent of total traffic, bounce rate,** and **conversion rate**. You can evaluate the success of promotional campaigns by looking at **AOV, value per customer,** and **order frequency** following the promotion. You can also test email subject lines by looking at **open rate** and review email performance by looking at **click-through rates** and **unsubscribe rates**.

Step 3: Develop the Scorecard and Campaign Reports

The Digital Branch team needs a more detailed scorecard. This scorecard tracks more KPIs and should reflect microevents and campaigns (marketing, advertising, customer service).

We recommend looking at your numbers in a twelve-month run rate, paying specific attention to

- the month, year over year;
- the previous month;
- the previous quarter; and
- the trends.

Sample Digital Branch Team Scorecard

	Owner	Goal (Week)	Week 1	Week 2	Week 3
Events					
Event 1	Sales				
Event 2	eCommerce		Online Sales Promotion Email Blast		
	eCommerce				
Revenue					
Total Revenue	Sales	$50,000	$45,000	$51,000	$60,000
eCommerce Revenue	eCommerce	$2,500	$2,250	$2,550	$3,000
eCommerce as a Percent Revenue	eCommerce	5%	3%	4%	5%
eCommerce Shipping Revenue	eCommerce	$460	$450	$500	$515
Adoption Funnel					
Registered Customers	Sales	10	15	8	12
Logins	eCommerce	200	201	250	190
Orders	eCommerce	100	90	150	105
# of Ordering Customers	eCommerce	75	80	81	90
Conversion Rate	eCommerce	3%	2.5%	2.0%	3.5%
First Orders	eCommerce	5	5	4	3
# of Repeat Orders	eCommerce	50	50	45	30
Average Order Value	eCommerce	$1,200	$1,001	900	$1,250
Abandoned Carts	eCommerce	25	30	35	15
Finance & Operations					
Product Gross Profit	Finance	$27,000	$24,750	$28,050	$33,000
Shipping Gross Profit	Finance	$125	$-500	$90	$145
Product Cost of Goods	Finance	$22,500	$20,250	$22,950	$27,000
Shipping Cost of Goods	Finance	$300	$400	$300	$275
Shipping Time	Operations	3 Days	3	4	4
Cash Days	Finance	15	20	25	14
Total Operating Expenses	Finance	$20,000	$19,000	$25,000	$27,000
Digital Marketing					
Website Users	eCommerce	550	600	450	500
Sessions	eCommerce	1,000	900	1,100	1,200
Page Views	eCommerce	10,000	15,000	9,000	10,000
Session Duration	eCommerce	4:00	4:30	3:50	4:25
Organic Traffic (% of total session)	eCommerce	75%	80%	70%	65%
Referral Traffic (% of total session)	eCommerce	20%	25%	15%	30%
Ad Traffic (# of sessions)	eCommerce	500	700	400	600
Email Subscribers New	eCommerce	5	4	3	6
Email Unsubscribe	eCommerce	3	5	6	2
Open Rate	eCommerce	20%	25%	19%	22%
Click Through Rate	eCommerce	10%	9%	11%	4%
Facebook Followers New	eCommerce	5	4	6	3
LinkedIn Followers New	eCommerce	3	3	2	1
Ad Spend (% of revenue)	eCommerce	5%	6%	4%	7%
Ad Conversion Rate	eCommerce	2%	1.5%	2.0%	1.8%
SEO Spend (% of revenue)	eCommerce	5%	4%	6%	5%
Blog Posts	eCommerce	5	4	3	5
Landing Pages	eCommerce	1	0	1	0
Customer Service					
Customer Service Emails	eCommerce	100	150	90	100
Hours to Response	eCommerce	5	8	10	5
Live Chat Sessions	eCommerce	200	250	200	190
Hours to Resolution	eCommerce	8	10	12	8
Overall Score (10 for above goal)			180	170	260

Key: ▨ Gray: below target   ■ Black: at or above target

Other Team Scorecards you can adopt:

- Customer Service (showing number, type, and time to resolve issues)
- Branch Managers (showing percent and sales of customers ordering online)

Sample Simple Campaign Report

Campain Name: Training Webinar	
DATE	12/15/2018
OWNER	eCommerce
DURATION	11/20/2018 - 12/1/2018
OWNER/S	Website, email, social media
PROMOTION	Free training webinar on new service
GOALS	100 signups, 25 live participants

Results	
TOTAL	95 signups, 20 live participants
WEBSITE	1500 unique page views, 45 signups
EMAIL	25% open rate, 5% click rate, 50 signups
SOCIAL MEDIA	150 post views, 20 likes, 0 signups

Details

Email subject lines:

Join our free WEBINAR (30% open rate)

You're invited: Free Webinar on new service (20% open rate)

Landing page:

https://mbywebsite.com/webinar

Step 4: Report Regularly

We recommend executives review their scorecard weekly, and we recommend the same for the Digital Branch team. Reporting should establish a basis for providing constructive feedback, developing new tactical approaches, and informing and driving new campaigns and website changes.

Your Action Plan

1. Create an Executive Scorecard as well as a Digital Branch Team Scorecard.
2. Make sure that one person is responsible for each line in the scorecard (one person may be responsible for many lines, but each line needs an owner).
3. Set up a weekly meeting to review the scorecards.
4. Develop your strategic planning and tactical direction from the scorecard content, campaign reports, and meeting insights.

CHAPTER 9

Operations

Getting Your Organization Set to Serve Your Customers

The final component in the X eCommerce System is operations. As in all components, the goal of operations is to **improve your customers' experience.** While traditionally operations have been in the job of making your business move more smoothly, we want to look at this function differently. How can you structure operations so that you can provide an exceptional customer experience? What are the levers you control that can make your business stand out?

To do this, your Digital Branch needs to be fully integrated into your business operations. Your online customers are often also your offline customers and advocates. Their experience with your business needs to be integrated: seamless, consistent, and positive. As we mentioned at the very start,

> *Customers are relatively simple, right? They interact with you, and they want the service that they are expecting to be delivered. What creates the complexity is the company.*

> **—Harald Fanderl**[17]

In this chapter, we review seven key operations that need to be working together for you to grow and learn from customers' experiences. If you haven't already adopted this perspective, here is your new mandate: **"What can we do independently and collaboratively to make our customers' work life simpler?"**

These sevens areas are depicted below:

The Concept of the Perfect Order

At B2X, we talk about the "perfect order." If you've ordered online, you've certainly experienced both perfect and imperfect orders:

- The perfect order—one that arrives on time, completed, with a clean invoice or packing slip, with any customer service questions responded to promptly and thoroughly, and with any returns handled easily and quickly
- The imperfect order—one that arrives late without notification or explanation, with parts missing or the wrong parts, and with a crumpled packing slip

As you've likely experienced, the perfect order builds trust, and with trust comes loyalty—you are more and more likely to purchase from a website that you know from experience will make your life easier.

Your operations must work in service of the perfect order, every time. Your customers want a convenient and straightforward experience. The progression from order placement to pickup to bill payment should be straightforward and simple. By aligning your seven operations, you can create a comprehensive approach for the perfect order throughout.

Case Study

A power transmissions and bearings company was launching their new site. In order to ensure internal and external adoption, the eCommerce team developed and led a number of internal trainings for inside sales and customer support, elevating the best sellers to be evangelists of the site.

To support customer adoption, the business developed educational videos for the website, customer webinars, and hands-on trainings at their customers' offices. For new site visitors, a pop-up training showed key areas on the website. After signing up to the email list, subscribers received a series of informational and education emails about the new features and functions of the site.

Takeaway

A programmatic approach to marketing and communications helped the business tell and retell the story and value of the new website, building customer anticipation and engagement. Through internal training and incentives, the team was ready and excited to help customers purchase through the site.

Customer Service

Customer service is focused on helping your customers solve their business problems. In brick and mortar, this is the in-person interaction, returns and exchanges, and account management. For your Digital Branch, you'll need the same, along with guidance on navigating your website.

(Bruce) Temkin's research has found that...customers actually want good customer service more than they want low prices...but companies often treat customer service as an unwanted stepchild.

— **MarketingProfs, "How to Keep Your Customer Experience Efforts on Track"[18]**

We look at customer experience in terms of the "perfect order"—a customer registers online easily; an online order is placed seamlessly, is fulfilled correctly, and is shipped without issue; and any returns or exchanges are handled smoothly.

A few things need to be put in place to achieve this:

- **Online customer service:** Email addresses and phone (ideally toll-free) numbers should be easy to find on the site. Also, consider live chat.

- **Expert customer service**: Staff should be trained and well versed in the website—where to find information, how to manage accounts, and how to place an order from start to finish.

- **Operational alignment with fulfillment**: The website should display accurate price and availability information, and once the order is placed, the right product needs to leave the right warehouse at the right time. How can quick shipment be offered? How quickly can orders be placed on a truck? Where can contract drivers be brought in to offer one- or two-day delivery?

- **Returns, exchanges, and refunds**: These activities need to be aligned with finance, fulfillment, and the warehouse.

- **Personal touch:** Where can your team build in a practice of providing a personal touch? Maybe it's a call after the first order or confirmation after a product exchange. When can your business employ the best of offline and online? Consider
  - personal follow-up emails;
  - personal phone calls;
  - thank-you notes; and
  - custom gifts/incentives.

Tools needed to achieve these include strong ERP integration, customer service resources to service online customers, and live-chat software.

Sales

Before you can "sell" your customers on the Digital Branch, you need to sell your sales team. Organizational alignment will be crucial to the success of your digital business. Recall our horror story at the beginning of the book about a sales team that undermined their company's eCommerce site by telling customers it would always be cheaper to buy directly from the reps themselves. There are ways to prevent that. You need an internal adoption plan that

- provides internal training and education to your sales team;
- develops commissions and incentive structures for online sales (note that if you want your digital business to be a bigger percentage of your overall revenue, you should incentivize online sales **more** than offline sales); and
- creates tools for your team to "sell" the site to your customers—engaging PDFs, PPTs, and webinars; swag; and specialized landing pages that can be easily shared.

Tools needed to achieve these include a customer relationship management (CRM) tool, iPads or other ways of showing the site on the road, a webinar platform, and digital and printed sales materials.

Marketing

This is your opportunity to do customer marketing—to communicate your unique value proposition, products, and services. Depending on the stage of your Digital Branch business, there are different marketing activities that can drive your customer education and engagement.

Start by segmenting your customers. Who are the readiest to adopt, and who are the most important to adopt? Target them first. For your biggest customers, build those relationships personally—communicate the benefits, and provide them access to education and information for every step of the way (how to register, how to search, how to order, how to place a return, etc.).

Here are some key efforts:

- Develop a marketing strategy (from your strategic plan) to drive Digital Branch growth:
  - Define your marketing goals.
  - Define your target audiences.
  - Define your mix of media/effort for your marketing activities.
  - Benchmark your competitors.
  - Define your online value proposition.
- Align branding with the website to promote the website and digital properties. Promote the website on packaging materials, swag, and all digital and print assets.

- Integrate digital marketing into your marketing operations and resources.

- Build a plan for key events, marketing campaigns, and product promotions (seasonal, category based, brand based, event specific, defined by margin).

- Develop a content marketing strategy, including blog articles, landing pages, webinars, email, and social media.

- Create automated programs (welcome and educational email marketing, on-site notifications).

- Build educational content (landing pages, videos, online tutorials, webinars/Facebook Live events).

- Foster and leverage partner relationships (building relationships with vendors, affiliated organizations or associations, and local charities or related organizations) for co-op marketing and advertising opportunities.

- Develop a customer loyalty program, incentivizing frequent and/or high-value purchasers.

- Manage your online community, engaging and interacting with customers and influencers online.

- Implement digital advertising (digital media, PPC, social media that aligns or compliments your print media).

- Understand and iterate based on user experience and analytics.

- Implement search engine optimization (SEO).

- Manage public relations with press releases, media relations, and events.

- Provide marketing reporting and analysis.

Tools needed to achieve these include brand guidelines, a marketing calendar, marketing software (including email), a webinar platform, and an online advertising management tool or individual platforms.

Your effort will also require creative support. You'll need to find or hire a strong writer and a strong designer to help create marketing campaigns that are clear, engaging, and branded to your business. These creative tasks include

- copywriting (web pages, landing pages, blog articles, emails, advertisements, social media);
- digital design (landing-page design, digital collateral such as ads and social media images);
- print design (collateral, print advertising, branded swag, etc.);
- user experience (UX) design (to support landing-page and website design changes);
- content management (to update and implement new changes to the website, such as adding new pages, uploading new images, performing copy edits); and
- website developers (both front end and back end to implement bigger website changes).

Tools needed to achieve these include Figma (web design and UX design tool), photo-editing tool (Figma or Photoshop), CMS, and an A/B testing tool (Optimizely).

Fulfillment

How are your orders packed and picked? How is shipping managed and optimized? Who ensures clear communication to branches for pickup?

Having the fulfillment process optimized means looking at

- inventory planning and management;
- supply chain and purchasing management;

- warehouse operations (ensuring accurate fulfillment and fast shipping);
- shipping provider management;
- brick-and-mortar branch integration (for returns or pickups);
- transparency about availability and fulfillment practices;
- shipping notifications and communications to customers; and
- managing customer expectations.

Tools needed to achieve these include a warehouse management system, ERP, and a fulfillment and shipping platform.

Information Technology (IT)

The perfect order has many dependencies on integrated information technology (IT), with your IT team working to ensure each component is working well both independently and together.

The systems include

- website hosting;
- ECommerce platform;
- ERP;
- ERP integration (API or other);
- email (internal and to customers);
- payment processing;
- analytics;
- PIM;
- marketing automation;

- notification/alert system (to notify customer service if orders have errors, when orders are picked, and when orders have shipped/been picked up); and

- other business tools such as accounting, customer relationship management (CRM), live chat, and video hosting.

Finance

How is your financial arm organized to drive your Digital Branch? Consider the following, for example:

- **Centralized pricing** (for company-wide price consistency)

- **Budget** (approval and understanding of technology costs in the immediate and near future as well as marketing budgets and hiring needs now and over time)

- **P&L** (understanding of the Digital Branch cost of business, margins, and opportunities)

Tools needed to achieve these include ERP or a centralized pricing tool, a budget tool or Excel for managing P&L, and an accounting system.

Human Resources

As we outlined in the **People** chapter, your Digital Branch is a resource-heavy enterprise. As you grow, you'll build more and more internal resources. This effort will require

- resource planning—understanding the gaps that need to be filled as well as how they will be filled today and over time;

- career-path planning—defining and communicating career paths for the team to support forward progress and resource retention;

- competitive benefits planning to attract valuable talent (What kind of benefits can you provide [in addition to excellent health coverage and 401Ks]? Consider paid time off, performance bonuses, paid volunteer time, educational stipends, company stock, flex time, paid family leave, remote work, etc.); and

- onboarding structure planning (to share company values and mission).

Tools needed to achieve these include onboarding materials (handbook), a competitive benefits package, and a resource management/planning tool.

Your Action Plan

1. Ensure centralized pricing and a strong relationship between your ERP and eCommerce platform.
2. Evangelize the site to your sales team.
3. Build your marketing resources, tools, and activities.
4. Align fulfillment, finance, and HR to understand where you are today and where you plan to be tomorrow.

CHAPTER 10

Five Phases of XES Maturity
From Foundation to Innovation

Wherever you are in your Digital Branch, these seven components are being well served or underserved within your organization. Whether you are starting from no eCommerce or gearing up to compete with the leading national players, the X eCommerce System will apply to your business.

In the following section, we look at the five phases of XES maturity and the business priorities to drive your Digital Branch.

This will set you well on your way to building a strategic, competitive, forward-looking Digital Branch. It's not easy, but it is doable, and you will be in good company with the other distributors who are making their way through this system.

Below are depicted the five phases of XES maturity:

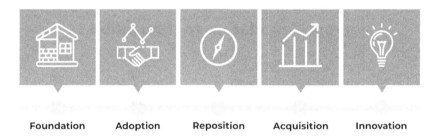

| Foundation | Adoption | Reposition | Acquisition | Innovation |

Phase 1: Foundation

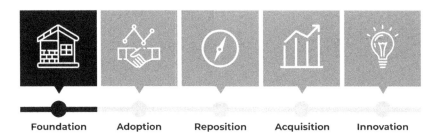

This is your first serious endeavor to drive eCommerce sales. In this phase, your eCommerce sales represent less than 10 percent of total revenue.

This is perhaps the most important phase, as it enables the rest of the phases to occur. In this phase, you will set the stage for your eCommerce growth by establishing a solid foundation to build upon.

	PRIORITIES
PLAN	The plan is the business case and the roadmap you will use to build from. Spend time and effort to build a comprehensive strategic plan that encompasses each element of the system: people, technology, UX, analytics, product content, and operations.
PEOPLE	Build a Digital Branch steering committee made up of at minimum a decision maker, IT leader, and business or marketing leader to provide governance and decision making in accordance with your plan. Your first order of duty is to hire an eCommerce leader (your Digital Branch manager). Start filling in other roles (product, customer service, and site

PEOPLE

management) with internal resources or lower-risk hires.

TECHNOLOGY

Select and implement your eCommerce platform, CMS (content management system), analytics, and basic marketing or email automation tools. Your analytics tools should include basic Google Analytics, Google Tag Manager, Enhanced eCommerce (a plug-in for Google Analytics), user ID ERP integration, and on-site search tracking. Select and implement your PIM or optimize your current PIM. Most distributors find it easier to implement their PIM first before implementing their eCommerce solution. However, both should be selected together to assure that the solutions can be integrated together.

PRODUCT CONTENT

Product content will be the fuel for your eCommerce site. Who will be in charge of product content? This should be an internal person who understands your products.

Start the process by defining your taxonomy and attribution design.

Source your product data. How will you acquire your product data? Vendors are typically not the single source. Most distributors use a third-party (often offshore) source to acquire their product data. Start with your stock items and expand from there.

Where will you store your product data? Your ERP typically isn't the ideal place to store product content.

PRODUCT CONTENT	Most distributors use or implement a PIM to store, aggregate, normalize, and enrich their product content as the single source of truth. Start building SKUs as well as rules and processes for content standards.
USER EXPERIENCE	This is a critical stage for user experience. Take great care to design out a foundational user experience that helps your customers do their job easier. The best way to start building your UX is to start journey mapping. Learn the process of journey mapping and incorporate this incredible tool into your UX process. UX is typically done prior to implementing your eCommerce platform and is a great way to build your requirements with your selected partner.
ANALYTICS	Set up scorecards for executives and the Digital Branch team. Establish customer-tracking analytics, on-site search, and product analytics reporting. Start by simply creating a scorecard based on the customer adoption or customer acquisition framework.
OPERATIONS	Start "selling" the Digital Branch internally, ensuring that sales, finance, and human resources are in alignment. Develop sales and marketing campaigns and materials. Build resource planning. Launch marketing campaigns (SEO, email marketing, webinars, and social media) as well as educational communications. Launch sales incentives for online sales.

Phase 2: Adoption

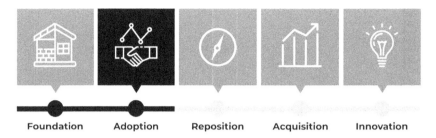

Your foundation is now in place. Now you can focus on getting your internal people to evangelize your Digital Branch, and on driving and deepening existing customer adoption. In this phase, your eCommerce sales are typically between 10 and 20 percent, and this phase is about pushing toward 30 percent of total revenue.

PRIORITIES	
PLAN	It is time to revise your plan to move beyond foundational and into adoption activities. Define your two-year plan for eCommerce adoption growth. What is the budget and human resourcing plan? What are the gaps?
PEOPLE	Seats you should have filled by now: ▪ eCommerce leader (Digital Branch manager) ▪ Product content manager ▪ Platform analyst Seats you should consider filling in this phase: ▪ Data analyst

- Digital marketing

PEOPLE

Continue to build your internal Digital Branch team, incorporating a dedicated product person, analytics support, and a dedicated, experienced marketing person. A data analyst is often needed in this phase to manipulate data from multiple sources.

Supplement with third parties for social, SEO, UX, and email marketing (as needed).

TECHNOLOGY

By this time, you have your eCommerce platform and CMS in place. Now it is time to think about marketing tools—marketing automation and email. In this stage, you also should make sure you have an on-site search optimization process in place to constantly optimize your search box and SERP (search engine results page) for on-site search.

In this stage, you should also start thinking about A/B testing tools.

PRODUCT CONTENT

Product content is a program, not a project. There is no such thing as perfect data, only improving data.

In the adoption phase, product content and on-site search begin to go hand in hand. Based on search analytics, build product content according to what analytics tell you to improve.

Build a system to test and learn from content, design, and UX performance, driven by analytics.

USER EXPERIENCE	Continue to incorporate journey mapping before any project. Journey mapping will put your customers at the center. UX improvements should be based on what issues you see from analytics. Often these improvements fall into the registration, "My Account," and checkout processes.
ANALYTICS	Review the scorecard and make changes as necessary to make it as understandable and actionable as possible. Use weekly meetings to drive change.
OPERATIONS	Ramp up customer marketing initiatives, including customer adoption and new-customer acquisition. Look at customer service and fulfillment to define opportunities to differentiate your business.

Phase 3: Reposition

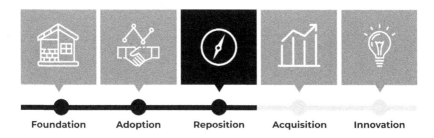

Foundation   Adoption   Reposition   Acquisition   Innovation

Building from the experience and knowledge of the previous phases, you look at opportunities to reposition your Digital Branch to best serve your current and potential customers. In this phase, your eCommerce sales are above 30 percent of total revenue, and you are now pushing toward 40 to 50 percent of total revenue. In this phase, we are building the foundation for phase 4: acquisition.

PRIORITIES	
PLAN	With more than 30 percent of revenue, you should now be able to sell further investment into this channel to your executive team. How will you use the investment? Where are your current gaps? Define your two-year plan for eCommerce growth. What is the budget and human resourcing plan? As always, create a road map to getting to phase 4. Set SMART goals.
PEOPLE	How has getting talent onto your team been going? By now, you should have the following seats filled: • eCommerce leader (Digital Branch manager) • Product content manager

PEOPLE	▪ Platform analyst ▪ Data analyst ▪ Digital marketing Consider hiring your own developers.
TECHNOLOGY	Often in this stage, it is time to redesign your site and update the UX as well as confirm you are using the right technology platforms. Review your eCommerce, CMS, on-site search, and PIM platforms. Search and CMS is often the place to make heavier investments. Look into advanced marketing automation tools.
PRODUCT CONTENT	Make sure you have a program in place to keep your product content fresh and unique. By now, you probably have product information that is out of date. Related products will help you build your average order value. Create a program to develop product up-sell, and cross-sell related products.
USER EXPERIENCE	Redesign your site to reposition for the upcoming acquisition phase. Think about a UX design for content marketing, SEO, blogs, and so on. Content marketing should be for optimization for Google and the other search engines.
ANALYTICS	Review the scorecard and make changes as necessary to make it as understandable and actionable as possible. Use weekly meetings to drive change.

OPERATIONS With a trusted Digital Branch in place, ramp up customer marketing initiatives, including customer adoption and new-customer acquisition. Look at customer service and fulfillment to define opportunities to differentiate your business.

Phase 4: Acquisition

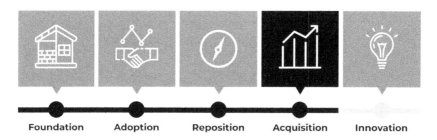

Foundation   Adoption   Reposition   Acquisition   Innovation

Now that you've built a site and organizational support for growth, your focus is on acquiring new customers and expanding the customer base. In this phase, eCommerce sales are typically over 60 percent of total revenue.

Acquisition, of course, isn't just about acquisition. It is really the intersection of adoption and acquisition. You have a solid foundation to deal with your existing customers and to bring new customers into the fold.

PRIORITIES	
PLAN	Continue your adoption plan, but now add a customer acquisition strategy. Focus on driving traffic and conversion rate optimization (CRO).
PEOPLE	You can now expand your team for acquisition. Digital marketing, SEO, social media reps, and copywriters are the key members to add to your team at this stage. Continue to build your development and technical resources.

TECHNOLOGY	Most B2B platforms can support B2C (guest buying) as well. Does your platform support what you need? Marketing automation will be key for this phase. Does your technology have the ability to test and track? Your UX will be about A/B testing and multivariate testing.
PRODUCT CONTENT	Look to big-picture opportunities for improvement and innovation, including style guides, image standards, and tools like discovery widgets. Continue to build your content program, focusing on unique data, cross-sell, and up-sell.
USER EXPERIENCE	In this phase, UX is about test, track, and optimize. Start by doing user testing, then use A/B testing and multivariate testing to continuously test new areas and ideas.

Phase 5: Innovation

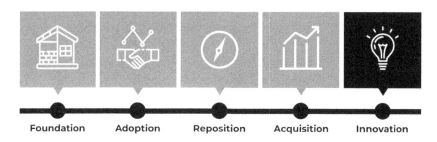

| Foundation | Adoption | Reposition | Acquisition | Innovation |

With an effective eCommerce site in place and data-driven optimization strategies under way, firms at this point are ready to begin looking beyond the known issues related to eCommerce and instead start designing and building ways to use digital technology to solve problems customers are not aware of, or for which they have never considered a technological solution. With eCommerce revenues representing over 75 percent of sales, this is often the phase where firms evolve from competition to disruption.

Now is the time to see where the business can innovate: What are the new technologies or new solutions that can be tested and implemented? Who are the people with the market research background and the technological experience to build new solutions? How do you build a culture of innovation in your team? How do you foster a "start-up" mentality within your organization that allows you to strive for long-term solutions, take risks, and leap past what your competitors are doing?

CHAPTER 11

Launching Your Digital Branch (for the First Time)
A Step-By-Step Guide

In this chapter, we'll break down eight steps to launching a site. You'll find the details involved in these steps in the earlier chapters, but this is our road map if you are just starting to launch or seriously relaunch your Digital Branch site.

Step 1: Priorities, Plans, and Roadmap

Define your business and technology needs for the site. B2B organizations are complex due to the dynamics surrounding customers, ordering processes, product mix, and internal systems. Because of this complexity, B2B companies need to build a digital customer experience that includes the following:

- ERP integration. This will likely represent a significant cost, both initially and in the long run. Tight integration between your eCommerce system and ERP is necessary to ensure that real-time inventory availability across warehouses, pricing per customer contract, order status, order history, and so on are presented accurately and consistently for each customer.
- Simplification of complex products and product relationships.
- Translation of complex customer ordering processes online.
- Extension of the sales and service relationships online.

Step 2: Technical Selection

If you visit each of the leading vendors' websites or listen to their webinars, you will realize how similar these software vendors sound. You might be confused at the end of those presentations. Most of the enterprise eCommerce vendors have been around for a while and have robust capabilities. However, some essential differences exist among the vendors that could affect your decision.

First, understand what is out of the box and what is customized. Often, the system demoed for you is a sales tool that has been heavily customized. After that, you'll want to understand the following key differentiators:

- Technology/Architecture
  - Java versus Microsoft
  - ERP integration (do they have experience with your ERP?)
- Search and navigation
- Personalization/segmentation
- Product information management (PIM/PCM)
- Business tools
- Time to market
- Road map/innovation
- "My Account" features and functions
- Ability to implement your technical, UX, and design requirements
- Price

Step 3: User Experience and Design

Start creating the user experience and design of your site. This should be a data-driven exercise, drawing from what you know about your customers, your business objectives, and the capacity of your selected platform.

If you have the time and capability, now is a good time to do a journey mapping exercise to articulate who your customer personas are and how your website can best serve them. Apply the knowledge you have from your current site, competitive analysis, and best practices to create a customer-centric UX and design. Strong technology and tight ERP integration are important; however, this must work hand in hand with a clean and intuitive UX and design.

Take the time to present your customers with a strong B2B online experience around the following areas of your site:

Home Page and Product Pages:

- Home page and navigation
- Product detail page
- Category page
- Search results
- All product categories
- All brands

Order Process:

- Shopping cart
- Checkout
- Quote management (request, view, convert)

Account Management:

- Registration
- My Account
- Open orders/order history
- Order detail
- Shipping addresses

Marketing/Static Pages:

- About Us
- Frequently Asked Questions (FAQs)
- Contact Us
- Locations page
- News and events
- Other static content-page templates

Mobile/Responsive:

Your site design should follow responsive web design practices, but here are the key screens to focus on a mobile-first approach:

- Home page
- Category page
- Product detail page
- My Account dashboard

Step 4: Implementation

After you've selected a platform vendor who is experienced and understands your business requirements, you then begin what will be a lengthy and expensive phase: implementation. You will need to have resources dedicated to project management of the site implementation and to test the site. These can be internal or external, but they should be in addition to the actual implementation partner(s).

Step 5: Testing

Before your site is ready to go to the public, now is the time to again test your site. Ideally you would have done some formative testing early in the design process to find any major issues before implementation. Now you must prove the effectiveness of your site design and prioritize any found issues as you move into the launch and postlaunch phases. With a small group of users—from your internal team, with select customers, or with a hired pool of testers—you can reveal usability issues and opportunities to provide clearer pathways, better design, or clarifying information. You will want to watch as your users complete some of your site's key tasks and functions. These include

- product search and find;
- correct and clear product information (images, information, and downloadable materials);
- checkout process;
- product detail page; and
- registration.

Step 6: Launch

Now that you finally have the site implemented, how do you get customers adopting (using) the site? It is not, as they say, "if you build it, they will come." For this phase, you will need to give people the information and a reason to be excited to visit your site. This can be implemented through

- internal training and communications;
- sales staff incentives;
- external communications and promotions, including a process for preregistering current customers;
- PR and marketing;
- customer service (e.g., email, phone, and live chat); and
- search engine optimization to drive organic search traffic to your site.

We outline a framework for customer adoption in the **Analytics** chapter.

Step 7: Ongoing Website Optimization

The benefit of your Digital Branch is that you can see in real time how your business is performing and why. Looking at your business plan, how is your site lining up with expectations? Looking at your scorecard, how is the site performing? Drawing from customer testing, surveys, and analytics, where can the site be improved? Ask yourself the following:

- What tools can be implemented to support an excellent customer experience (e.g., live chat, email marketing, or on-site notifications)?

- What user experience can be tweaked to make it easier for customers to find products and check out? (We go into this in more detail in the **Product Content** chapter.)

- What design changes can make your site easier to scan quickly for information?

- What content and marketing campaigns (email, print, SEO, social media) can help educate, inform, and delight your customers and drive them to purchase?

Importantly, you also need to

- create a calendar to plan marketing and content activities; and

- test and learn from new campaigns and initiatives.

Step 8: Driving New Business

We think of this like building a house before inviting new guests in. Once your house is built, the trim is done, the fixtures are installed, the floor is finished, and the pictures are hung, that's when you can invite new people over. Having implemented, launched, and optimized your site, now you are ready to start focusing on driving new traffic to your website. Start with a plan, defining your target audiences, budget, and ROI. From there, create audience-specific content (webinars, landing pages, email, and ad campaigns). Then develop creative ad campaigns (PPC, media, and social media). Finally, launch, manage, and monitor your ad campaign.

CHAPTER 12

Getting Started
Focus on Your Customers and Get in the Game

The XES is a special system. Used properly, this system and the tools provided will transform your organization. At the core, though, this whole endeavor is all about your customers. Help make their job easier, and they will come back to your Digital Branch time and time again.

Finally, I sincerely believe that the internet is the great equalizer. You aren't behind...yet. Every company, big or small, has the opportunity to use the internet to create an experience for its customers that adds tremendous value.

You must put your customers in the middle of your process, and you must brainstorm ways to give them tools that will help them do their job more easily. Then test, analyze, optimize, and repeat.

Organizations that decide to use digital to create a unique customer experience will be the ones left standing a few years down the line. You don't have to spend millions of dollars to get there. But you do have to start.

Justin King

Notes

[1] McKinsey, "Why the customer experience matters," May 2016: https://www.mckinsey.com/business-functions/marketing-and-sales/our-insights/why-the-customer-experience-matters

[2] Amazon, "Amazon Jobs," *https://www.amazon.jobs/working/working-amazon* (August 2018)

[3] Papke, Edgar, *True Alignment: Linking Company Culture with Customer Needs for Extraordinary Results* (AMACOM; Special ed. Edition, December 11, 2013), 17.

[4] Human Element, "FIRO theory," https://thehumanelement.com/pages/firo-theory/ (August 2018)

[5] Edgar Papke, "Understanding the customer experience: part two," http://edgarpapke.com/2018/02/07/understanding-the-customer-experience-2/ (August 2018)

[6] Papke, Edgar, *True Alignment: Linking Company Culture with Customer Needs for Extraordinary Results* (AMACOM; Special ed. edition (December 11, 2013), 36.

[7] Cuban, Mark, *How to Win at the Sport of Business: If I Can Do It, You Can Do It* (Diversion Books, 2011), 81.

[8] Bluesoft Labs, "Try an Internal Press Release before starting new Products" https://medium.com/bluesoft-labs/try-an-internal-press-release-before-starting-new-products-867703682934 (August 2018)

[9] Jim Collins, "Good to Great," https://www.jimcollins.com/article_topics/articles/good-to-great.html (August 2018)

[10] Accenture, "Building The B2B OmniChannel Commerce Platform Of The Future B2B Buyer Expectations Are Driving Sellers To Deliver Fully Functional Omni-Channel Experiences," https://www.accenture.com/us-en/_acnmedia/Accenture/Conversion-Assets/DotCom/Documents/Global/PDF/Dualpub_1/Accenture-Building-Omni-Channel-Commerce-Platform-Future.pdf (August 2018)

[11] Parry, Tim, "B2B Suppliers Are Investing in Ecommerce," *Multichannel Merchant*, http://multichannelmerchant.com/ecommerce/b2b-suppliers-investing-ecommerce/#_ (August 2018)

[12] Lyons, Daniel, "'We Start With the Customer and We Work Backward.' Jeff Bezos on Amazon's success." *Slate Magazine*, December 24, 2009 http://www.slate.com/articles/news_and_politics/newsmakers/2009/12/we_start_with_the_customer_and_we_work_backward.html

[13] Reland, Brett, "Why Customer Engagement Is the Future of Ecommerce," *Entrepreneur.com*, January 13, 2015 https://www.entrepreneur.com/article/241268

[14] "Kaplan, Robert, *The Balanced Scorecard: Translating Strategy into Action* (Harvard Business Review Press, August 2, 1996)

[15] Hinshaw, Michael, "The Real Value In Voice Of The Customer: The Customer Experience," *CMO.com*, March 29, 2016 http://www.cmo.com/opinion/articles/2016/3/29/the-real-value-in-voice-of-the-customer-the-customer-experience.html#gs.9f4JBss

[16] Nielsen, Jakob, "Why You Only Need to Test with 5 Users," *Nielsen Norman Group,* March 19, 2000 https://www.nngroup.com/articles/why-you-only-need-to-test-with-5-users/

[17] McKinsey, "Why the customer experience matters," May 2016: https://www.mckinsey.com/business-functions/marketing-and-sales/our-insights/why-the-customer-experience-matters

[18] MarketingProfs, "How to Keep Your Customer Experience Efforts on Track" http://www.marketingprofs.com/short-articles/1834/how-to-keep-your-customer-experience- (August 2018)

About B2X Partners

B2X Partners is a full-service digital B2B eCommerce agency focused on driving digital business for distributors and manufacturers.

With over thirty years of industry experience, B2X Partners brings insights, expertise, and best practices to complex B2B business challenges in a way that is practical, profitable, and focused on sustainable success.

At B2X Partners, we are passionate about helping distributors, and manufacturers create profitable, competitive digital businesses.

For more free training, articles, information and our podcast and events, please visit our website: **www.b2xpartners.com**

About the Authors

Justin King

With almost twenty years working in eCommerce, Justin King has been on the forefront of the growth and trends in B2B eCommerce.

Justin is CEO at B2X Partners and works with customers to help them understand and build eCommerce strategies that are visionary, tactical, and meaningfully impactful to their business. In addition to providing strategy and execution insights to his clients, Justin is a leading speaker on B2B customer experience and eCommerce. Prior to B2X, Justin was chief evangelist, B2B eCommerce, at Oracle Corporation, where he built the go-to-market strategy for Oracle's B2B eCommerce product. Justin previously held executive roles at software companies Endeca/hybris and eCommerce agencies Rosetta and Brulant.

- **Email:** justin.king@b2xpartners.com
- **LinkedIn:** https://www.linkedin.com/in/justinking/

Sarah Falcon

 Sarah Falcon is a digital marketing professional with over ten years' experience driving measurable growth, customer acquisition, engagement, and retention. At B2X Partners, Sarah works with customers to develop impactful eCommerce marketing and communications strategies for measurable growth. Throughout her career, she has worked with start-ups and nonprofits as well as a number of B2B distributors to analyze, develop, implement, and execute integrated marketing strategies and campaigns.

- **Email:** sarah.falcon@b2xpartners.com
- **LinkedIn:** https://www.linkedin.com/in/sarahfalcon/

Jason Hein

 With over twenty years of experience with B2B merchandising, Jason is proud to have helped firms of all sizes achieve excellence online. Prior to consulting, his career highlights include working with McMaster-Carr during its eCommerce transition and building the original content team that helped launch Amazon Supply. He is a noted speaker and B2B eCommerce evangelist, having spoken for organizations such as the NAW (National Association of Wholesalers) and ISA (Industrial Supply Association), as well as contributor to webinars for *Modern Distribution Magazine* and *Industrial Distribution* magazine.

- **Email:** jason.hein@b2xpartners.com
- **LinkedIn:** https://www.linkedin.com/in/jasonhein/

Ashley Lillis

Ashley Lillis is a seasoned eCommerce strategist with over twelve years of experience. As a member of the B2X team, Ashley worked with small and midsized distributors, helping them with strategy, UX, digital marketing, and analytics. Prior to B2X, Ashley was with Rosetta, an interactive marketing agency, where she focused on developing eCommerce strategies for large retailers and B2B clients.

- **Email:** ashley.lillis@b2xpartners.com
- **LinkedIn:** https://www.linkedin.com/in/ashley-lillis-3013235/

Kristen Lohman

Kristen is a User Experience Designer with a unique skill set of user research, interaction design, and user interface design and a background in both writing and visual design. She has worked in the private and public sector, designing websites and applications that combine user, business, and development goals. At B2X, she strives to match clients' objectives with the needs of their target audience to enhance the user experience throughout the customer life cycle.

- **Email:** kristen.lohman@b2xpartners.com
- **LinkedIn:** https://www.linkedin.com/in/kristenalohman/

INDEX

33299696R00083

Made in the USA
Columbia, SC
08 November 2018